Algrove Publishing Limited
1090 Morrison Drive
Ottawa, Ontario
Canada K2H 1C2

Canadian Cataloguing in Publication Data

Henderson, Peter, 1822-1890
    Gardening for pleasure

(Classic reprint series)
3rd ed.
Originally published: New York : Orange Judd, 1883.
ISBN 0-921335-79-2

    1. Gardening. I. Title. II. Series: Classic reprint series (Ottawa, Ont.)

SB93.H45 2000   635   C00-900161-1

Printed in Canada
#10300

Publisher's Note

Peter Henderson was the author of a number of gardening books in the late Victorian era. His works were originally published by the Orange Judd Company, which did a large number of "How To" books of that period, but his works were so popular he eventually started his own publishing company. He probably did more than any other author to popularize market gardening. Some other titles of his include *Gardening for Profit, Practical Floriculture, Handbook of Plants and General Horticulture, Gardening Guide and Record, Farm and Garden Topics,* and *How the Farm Pays.* All of his books are soundly based in the economics of the activity, and give excellent practical advice on a variety of gardening subjects.

Leonard G. Lee, Publisher
March, 2000
Ottawa

Gardening for Pleasure.

A GUIDE TO THE AMATEUR IN THE

FRUIT, VEGETABLE, AND FLOWER GARDEN,

WITH FULL DIRECTIONS FOR THE

GREENHOUSE, CONSERVATORY, AND WINDOW-GARDEN.

BY

PETER HENDERSON,

AUTHOR OF "GARDENING FOR PROFIT," AND "PRACTICAL FLORICULTURE,"
JERSEY CITY HEIGHTS, N. J.

ILLUSTRATED.

NEW YORK:
ORANGE JUDD COMPANY,
751 BROADWAY.
—
1883.

CONTENTS.

———◆◇◆———

(3)

INTRODUCTION.

I have endeavored in writing " Gardening for Pleasure," to divest it, as far as I was competent to do so, of the technical terms and phrases which professional gardeners use in writing or talking on matters relating to horticulture ; and to use the plainest language at my command in describing the simplest methods of culture. Whether I have succeeded in making the subject as clear as I have desired to do, those who read the work must decide.

My aim in writing the book was to make it such as would be useful to the occupant of a city lot, or to the possessor of a few window plants, as well as to the owner of a country residence that is fully appointed in all matters relating to the cultivation of flowers, fruits, and vegetables. The necessity for such a book has been made evident to me by the inquiries from hundreds of amateurs in gardening ; inquiries to many of which neither of my previous works, ("Gardening for Profit," or "Practical Floriculture,") furnished proper replies ; the one being written mainly for information of the vegetable market gardener, and the other for the commercial florist.

PETER HENDERSON.

Jersey City, N. J., Oct., 1875.

(7)

Gardening for Pleasure

CHAPTER I.

SOIL AND LOCATION.

It is rare in determining the site for a residence, that the soil is taken into consideration, and in consequence, we sometimes find that the garden surrounding the house presents a barren appearance, that nothing can remedy short of the placing a foot of good soil over the whole surface. This condition is not so often due to the natural poverty of the soil, as caused by grading off the surface soil, or by filling up to the desired grade with the material thrown out in excavating the cellars, or other subsoil, clay, or gravelly material, and placing these over the soil intended for the garden. This is often done for the convenience of contractors, to the great injury of the proprietor, without either being aware of the bad results. As a good soil will tend more than all else to give satisfactory results in garden operations, it is all important to secure it. When discretion can be used in deciding on a location, one should be chosen that has naturally a suitable soil, rather than to attempt to make it so by carting a foot of good soil over the bad, which would be found not only very expensive, but in many situations, next to impracticable. I have

(9)

before said, in some of my writings on this subject, that the soil best suited for all garden purposes, is what is known as "sandy loam," not less than ten inches deep, overlying a subsoil of sand or gravel. Such a soil rarely requires drainage, is easier worked, and gives better results than that known as " clayey loam," which overlays a putty-like subsoil of blue or yellow clay, which must be drained thoroughly before a seed is sown or plant set out, or there will be no satisfactory reward for the labor. The location, if choice can be made, should be such as will allow the garden to slope gently, (say one foot in a hundred), to the south or south-east, and if protected by hills or timber to the north-west, so much the better. If not protected naturally, a hedge of Hemlock Spruce, or Norway Firs, planted on the northern and western side of the site intended for the garden, would be of great advantage. These evergreens can be bought from 2 to 3 feet high, at from $15 to $25 per 100 ; and should be planted according to size, from 2 to 3 feet apart, making a cheap and ever improving screen or fence, which may be trimmed to any required hight or thickness.

CHAPTER II.

DRAINAGE.

As drainage will be in many instances indispensable to success, I will briefly state a few of the simplest methods that may be adopted, premising that it is utterly useless to expect to cultivate any soil satisfactorily that does not freely and rapidly carry off the surface water. An expert in soils can determine almost to a certainty by digging down two or three feet, whether or not a soil requires drainage, but the safest guide for the inexperienced is to judge by the growing crops in his neighborhood. If on a similar soil good crops of corn, potatoes, or hay, are found on undrained soil, then it is certain there is no necessity to drain, for no matter how cultivated, or how heavily manured land is, there can never be a good crop raised in any season, if the soil is water-logged. If the place to be drained is of large extent, and the ground nearly level, it will always be safer to call in the services of an engineer to give the proper levels and indicate the necessary fall, which should never

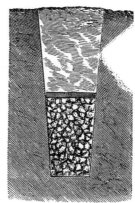

Fig. 1.—RUBBLE DRAIN.

be less than half a foot in the hundred, and if more can be had, so much the better. In heavy, clayey soils, we make our lateral drains three feet deep and fifteen feet apart, where there is less clay in the subsoil, we make them from twenty to thirty feet apart, and four feet deep. If stones are plenty on the ground, they may be profitably used in filling up the excavated ditch to half its depth, as shown in figure 1, and which is known as a rubble drain, using the larger stones at the bottom, and

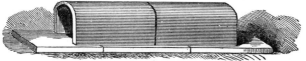

Fig. 2.—HORSE-SHOE DRAIN-TILE.

smaller at top, and covering over with inverted sods, to keep the soil from being washed in among the stones, and thus choking up the drain. But when they can be obtained at reasonable price, the best and most durable draining is that done by tiles. It makes but little difference whether the tile used is the round with collars, or the horse-shoe; we rather prefer the latter, particularly if the bottom of the drain is " spongy ; " we then use a board for the bottom of the drain, as shown in figure 2. This board is a common one of hemlock or spruce, cut in four pieces ; it is ripped through the middle, and then these parts split in two, making boards of five inches wide by half an inch in thickness, thus making the common hemlock board stretch out to a length of fifty feet. It is often a very troublesome matter to get the few drain tiles necessary to drain a small garden, and in such cases an excellent and cheap substitute can be had by using one of boards. Take ordinary rough boards, pine, hemlock, or spruce, and cut them into widths of three or four inches, nail them together so as to

Fig. 3.—TRIANGULAR BOARD DRAIN.

form a triangular pipe, as represented in figure 3, taking care to " break the joints " in putting the lengths together ; care must be taken that the boards are not nailed together too closely, else they might swell so as to prevent the water passing into the drain to be carried off. These drains are usually set with a flat side down, but they will keep clear better, if put with a point down, though it is more trouble to lay them. Drains made in this way will last much longer than might be supposed. Last season I came across some wooden drains that I had put down over twenty years before, and they seemed sound enough to last twenty years longer.

CHAPTER III.

PREPARATION OF THE GROUND

After draining, (if draining is necessary), comes the preparation of the soil. Presuming that the ground where the new garden is to be made is an open space, clear of trees or other obstructions, there is no cultivation so cheap and yet so thorough, as plowing and harrowing. To do this properly, the ordinary plow should be followed by the subsoil plow, stirring the subsoil up about fifteen inches deep, so that the water will pass through to the drains, natural or artificial, freely. After the plow and subsoiler, follows the harrow, which should be weighted, so that the teeth sink six inches into the soil, in order to completely pulverize it. In Europe, it would be considered sacrilege to use a plow or harrow in the preparation of a private garden, and most of old-country gardeners among us will stand aghast at such advice, but I have been through all parts of the work, and am well satisfied, from no limited practice, that plowing and harrowing will not only do the work at one-fourth of the cost, but in a better manner than the ordinary digging or trenching with the spade. Let me here caution that great care be taken never to plow, dig, harrow, rake, or hoe ground when wet; if work must be done, pull out weeds, or set plants, if you will, but never, under any circumstances, stir the soil in preparation for a crop until it is dry enough not to clog. If stirred while wet, the particles stick together, and the crop is not only injured for the season, but in some soils the bad effects show for years.

CHAPTER IV.

WALKS.

It is no unusual thing to see the owner of a neat cottage make himself perfectly ridiculous by the way in which he lays out the walk from the street to his front door. There is a prevailing opinion that such walks should be curved ones, and gentlemen, often otherwise shrewd and intelligent, place themselves without question in the hands of some self-styled "garden architect," and thus manage to make themselves the laughing stock of a neighborhood. There was a well marked instance of this in a garden occupying a block in almost the center of Jersey City, where a man pretending to have a full knowledge of the subject, induced the proprietor to have a walk running about one hundred yards from the street to the house, made so curved that its length was nearly twice that distance. It was hard on the butcher's and grocer's boys, and it was said that even book-peddlers and sewing-machine agents, and lightning-rod men, looked ruefully at it and left him in peace. Some old authority on this subject says, that there "never should be any deviation from a straight line unless from some real or apparent cause." So if curved lines are insisted on, a tree, rock, or building must be placed at the bend as a reason for going around such obstacles. It will be evident to any one who reflects upon the matter, that a curved walk running a distance of a hundred yards or so from the street to the house, across an unplanted lawn, is utterly absurd. All short foot-walks from the street to the house should be straight, entering from the street at as near right angles as possible, and leading direct to the front door. There should be no necessity for a carriage road to the front entrance of a house, unless it is distant

at least 100 feet from the street, and then a drive is best
made by having an entrance at each side of the lot, as
given in figure 4, presuming that the width of the
ground is 500 feet, and the distance from street to the
front door is 150 feet. Even here the foot-walk should
be direct. The width of the roads or walks must be
governed by the extent of the grounds. For carriage-
way the width should not be less than ten feet, and for
foot-walks, five feet. Nothing is more annoying than to
have a shower-bath in early morning from the dew from

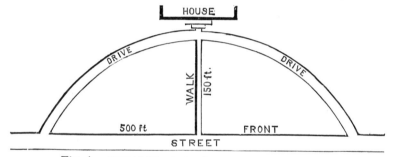

Fig. 4.—APPROACH TO A HOUSE—DRIVE AND PATH.

an overhanging branch in your narrow walk. We often
see gardens of considerable pretentions where the walks
are not more than three feet wide, where it is utterly impossible for two persons to walk abreast without getting
their dresses torn or faces scratched by overhanging
branches. Besides, it argues a narrowness in the
owner, particularly if the grounds are at all extensive,
and looks as if he were determined to cultivate every
available foot of land. Of course it is another matter
when the garden plot is limited to the width of a city
lot, (20 or 25 feet) ; then such economy of space is perfectly excusable. The character of the soil must in a
great measure determine the manner of making the road.
Every one must have noticed that after a heavy rain, un-
paved streets in some districts remain next to impassable
for many hours, while in others, after the same amount

of rain, the roads will seem firm and comparatively dry. In the former all carriage roads, and even foot-walks, to have any satisfaction from them, should have their foundations formed something like that shown in figure 5 ; this gives thorough drainage for the water at each side, and a depth of from one foot at center to two feet on sides of rubble stone and gravel to form the bed of the road or walk ; but in sandy or gravelly soils, through which the

Fig. 5.—SECTION OF ROAD WITH DRAIN EACH SIDE.

water passes quickly, no such expense is necessary, as an equally good road may be made by five or six inches of gravel. In foot-walks on such soils, I have found that three or four inches of gravel mixed with one fourth its bulk of cement to "bind," when watered and well rolled, makes an excellent smooth walk, and one in which, because of its hardness, there is no trouble with weeds.

CHAPTER V.

MANURES.

Whether one wishes to cultivate vegetables, fruits, or flowers, all soils, to give good results, sooner or later need manure ; this is more particularly the case with what are known as "vegetables," these being usually quick growing, succulent plants. No "fertilizer" answers so well for all purposes as thoroughly decayed stable manure, whether from horse or cow stable, it makes but little difference, except that that from the horse stables is best suited for heavy soils, while that from the cow-stables suits best for light soils. The quantity used for vegetables should not be less than would cover the whole surface of the ground at least three inches deep, and it should be mixed with the soil as thoroughly as possible by plowing or spading. In the absence of stable manure, recourse must be had to concentrated fertilizers, the best of which are Peruvian guano and bone dust. Here a word of caution is necessary as to the quantity to be used ; as their fertilizing qualities are concentrated, instead of being diffused as in stable manure ; if either guano or bone dust, or fertilizers of similar character, come directly in contact in large quantities, with the roots of plants, it injures them beyond remedy, hence in the use of these the necessity for caution. In our large field practice in vegetable growing, we use about 2,000 lbs. per acre of guano, sowing it on the surface of the ground after plowing, and then harrowing it in so as to mix it with the soil to the depth of five or six inches. Now, as there are 4,840 square yards in an acre, it will be seen that something more than half a pound of guano or bone dust is required for every square yard of surface to be fertilized. This quantity will just nicely cover the surface, about as thick as the sand on a sanded floor ; after spreading on the dug surface, it should be mixed with the soil with a spading fork or long-toothed rake to the depth of five or six inches, bearing in mind that the more thoroughly it is mixed with the soil the better will be the result. If used in "hills" for corn, tomatoes, melons, etc., the same proportionate quantity is to be applied, and the mixing must be equally thorough.

CHAPTER VI.

HOW TO USE CONCENTRATED FERTILIZERS.

Whatever kind of concentrated fertilizer may be used, I find it well repays the labor to prepare it in the following manner: to every bushel of fertilizer, add three bushels of either leaf-mold (from the woods), well pulverized muck, sweepings from a paved street, or—in the absence of either of the above—common garden soil. In every case the material employed must be as dry as it is possible to procure it. When guano is used, be careful to have it thoroughly pulverized and broken up before mixing with the other ingredients. The fertilizer must be well mixed with the soil or mold used by turning it at least twice. This mixing should be done in winter, or early spring, and the material packed away in barrels in a dry place for at least a month before using it. The main object of this operation is for the better separation and division of the fertilizer, so that when applied, it can be more regularly distributed over the land ; besides this, no doubt the fertilizing qualities of the leaf-mold or other substance are developed by this treatment. Experiment has shown that this method of using concentrated fertilizers of nearly all kinds, materially increases their value. One of the most successful market-gardeners in our neighborhood, has adopted this method for years, and in extensive experiments with different kinds of fertilizers, with and without being mixed, finds a saving of quite one-third in quantity in thus treating them. He finds that 1,200 lbs. of guano, mixed with two tons of garden soil, and sown over the surface after plowing, and then harrowed in, is equal in effect to 2,000 lbs. of guano used without mixing.

We have ourselves experimented with guano, blood and bone, and bone flour, with nearly like results, and as a top dressing for grass, we think the advantage of mixing is even more marked.   When fertilizers are applied to corn, potatoes, tomatoes, etc., in hills or drills, it is not only more economical to mix in this manner, but much safer in inexperienced hands ; for when any strong fertilizer is used pure, injury is often done to the roots by their coming in contact with it in too great quantity in the raw state, owing to imperfect mixing in the hill or drill, while, if composted as advised above, the danger is much less.   We are often asked as to the quantity to be applied to different garden crops.   Taking guano as a basis, we would recommend for all vegetable crops, if earliness and good quality are desired, the use of not less than 1,200 lbs. per acre, (an acre contains 4,840 square yards, and cultivators for private use can easily estimate from this the quantity they require for any area), mixed with two tons of either of the materials recommended. This quantity is used broadcast by sowing on the ground after plowing, and deeply and thoroughly harrowing in, or if in small gardens, forked in lightly with the prongs of a garden fork or long toothed steel rake.   When applied in hills or drills, from 100 to 300 lbs. should be used to the acre, according to the distance of these apart, mixing with soil, etc., as already directed.

In regard to which of the fertilizers is most desirable, we find but little difference, provided each is pure.   Guano at $80 per ton, is relatively as cheap as blood and bone fertilizer at $65 ; bone flour at $50, or superphosphate at $40 ; for in the lower priced articles we find we are obliged to increase the quantity to obtain the same results, so that the cost is nearly alike whichever be used.   The all important point is the purity of the article, a matter that few working farmers or gardeners ever attempt to decide except by the results in culture, hence we advise each one who has been using a fertilizer that has proved satisfactory, to experiment but lightly with another until the new article has proved its merits. The competition in the manufacture of articles so much in use as fertilizers, has in many instances forced down prices below the point at which they can be produced in a pure state, hence the widespread adulteration with " salt cake," " plaster," and other articles utterly worthless but to make weight. Next in meanness to the quack that extracts money from a poor consumptive for his vile nostrums, is the man who compels the poor farmer or gardener, may be a thousand miles away struggling for an existence, to pay freight on the sand mixed with his guano, or the plaster in his bone dust. In this relation I am reminded of a retribution that fell on the " Sands of Life man," who figured so conspicuously a few years ago in New York. The advertisement of this philanthropic gentleman, it will be remembered, was that " A retired clergyman whose Sands of Life had nearly run out," would for a consideration tell how the " running out " could be stopped in others. A kind hearted fellow in Illinois, deeply sympathizing with the old gentleman on account of his loss of " sand," sent him by express— but forgot to prepay—a thousand pounds of the article ! It is reported that the " retired clergyman " on opening the cask, expressed himself in a manner not only ungrateful, but utterly unclerical. We counsel no vengeance, but if some of these sand-mixing guano men could have the sand sifted out by their victims with compound interest added, and returned to them under the fostering care of an express company, it would be but even handed justice,

CHAPTER VII.

SPECIAL FERTILIZERS FOR PARTICULAR PLANTS.

A man called at my office a few years ago with some dozen bottles as samples of special manures, indispensable, he said, as fertilizers for certain kinds of plants. He had those with him that he claimed to be specially prepared for cabbage, corn, potatoes, wheat, grass, lawns, beets, etc., etc. He even invaded Flora's realm, and declared that his nostrum for roses was a specific for any languid capers of this sometimes rather coquettish queen of flowers. His own arguments, which were rather plausible and glibly uttered, were backed up by numerous certificates—authentic, I have no doubt—where his "potato fertilizer" had worked wonders with some, with others his "corn manure" had been of undoubted benefit, and so on all through the list.

Now, I have no reason to say that the vender of these fertilizers was a quack, except the broad fact, gathered from an experience of thirty years, that has shown me that it makes but little difference with what fertilizer a crop is treated, provided the soil is properly pulverized and the fertilizer applied in proper proportions according to its strength. Had all his separate kinds of fertilizers been taken from the same bag, (provided that bag contained a good article of bone-dust or guano), the result to his patrons would have been the same, whether he had used it on one or all of the crops that he had special prescriptions for.

There are few market gardeners in the vicinity of New York but who have at one time or another been obliged to take anything they could get for fertilizing purposes, and the difference has never been perceptible when manure from horse stables or cow stables has been applied,

or when $100 per acre has been expended for bone-dust
or Peruvian guano, and these all used on a dozen different crops without any discrimination.   Agricultural
chemistry may be all very well in some respects, but if
it gets down to such hair-splitting niceties as to analyze
scores of special plants, and tell us that we must feed
each with only just such food as the analysis show it to be
composed of, then our common sense, born of practical
experience, must scout and ridicule such nonsense.

Plants, like animals, are not so much kept in good
health by the special kind of food given as by the proper
quantity and conditions surrounding the individual when
the food is received, and what proper temperature and
pulverization of soil may be to the plant, air and exercise
and also proper temperature are the corresponding conditions necessary for healthy animal life.   Who will say
that the beef-fed English laborer is in any way the physical superior of the Irishman or Scotchman whose daily
food has been only potatoes and oat-meal ?   You get
usually fine and nearly equal development in each case,
but it is a condition due to a natural use of the muscles
in the open air in a congenial climate rather than to
anything special in the food.   It would be quite as reasonable to tell us that a special food, chemically considered, is necessary for each class of our domestic animals
as for our domestic plants, and none but the veriest
charlatan or ignoramus will do either.

CHAPTER VIII.

THE LAWN.

Since the introduction of the lawn-mowers, the keeping of the lawn has been so simplified that no suburban
residence is complete without one, and there is now no

more excuse for tall grass " going to hay" in the door
yard than there would be for cobwebs taking possession of
the rooms inside the dwelling. We occasionally see some
parsimonious individual, even now, who remembers that
in his grandfather's days, grass was allowed to grow for
the food of the "critters," and he leaves it for food for
his "critters" still. Though at the same time his furniture
inside, that nobody but himself ever sees, or has an opportunity to admire, for such men are not troubled with
friends, may have cost him $5,000 or $10,000. We have
two or three notable examples of this kind in my immediate neighborhood, but it is gratifying to know that
such neighbors are not numerous, for the example of
the majority will soon shame them into decency. To
have a lawn in first rate condition, the ground must be
put in order in the way described under the heads of
" Draining " and " Preparation of the Soil," for if these
are necessary anywhere, they are still more necessary for
the lawn, the soil of which should be as thoroughly pulverized and enriched by manure, as any ground intended
for the cultivation of either vegetables or fruits.

Great care must be taken to have the surface of the
ground for the lawn, (unless a very large one), made
perfectly level, for if this is not done before the lawn
is sown, it cannot be altered but at great expense
and inconvenience. After the surface is made level
roughly, it should be further smoothed with the rake,
and all stones of any considerable size removed, so that
the surface will be smooth for the action of the lawn-
mower. Wherever the extent of the lawn does not exceed 2,500 square feet, and where sods can be obtained
from a suitable pasture near at hand without much cost,
the best way to make the lawn is to sod it, but before
doing so, the ground should be rolled or beaten down,
particularly if any portion of it has been filled in, so that
there may be no " settling " to form hollows or inequali-

ties. A convenient size of sod to lay down is 12 by 18 inches, and of a thickness of 2 inches, in laying see that the edges are neatly laid together; and the whole firmly beaten down with the back of a spade. If it is dry weather when the work is done, it may be necessary to thoroughly drench the newly-laid sod for a week or so after planting, every other evening. When the lawn is too extensive to be sodded, the following mixture of grass seed may be used, which we have found to make an excellent lawn :

> 8 quarts Rhode Island Bent Grass.
> 3 quarts Creeping Bent Grass.
> 10 quarts Red Top Grass.
> 10 quarts Kentucky Blue Grass.
> 1 quart White Clover.

This mixture is not indispensable to the formation of a good lawn, though we believe it to be the best. Some of the fine lawns seen at Newport, R. I., are composed almost entirely of Rhode Island Bent grass mixed with about one-sixth of white clover, but the humidity of the atmosphere there has no doubt more to do with the richness of the lawn than the variety of grass it is composed of. I may here caution the use of spurious seed for this purpose. It is no uncommon thing that either through ignorance or short-sighted economy, "hay-seed" is taken direct from the hay-loft and sown to form the lawn. If from good hay, the seed will be principally timothy and red clover, and vain would be all the attempts to get a smooth lawn from such a source. It would be about as reasonable to expect figs from thistles. If the soil is rich, and has been thoroughly prepared, three bushels per acre will be sufficient, but if thin and poor, from four to five bushels had better be sown. If sown in early spring, as soon as the soil is dry enough to work, a good lawn will be formed by midsummer the first year, if it has been mown regularly at intervals of eight or ten days. The seed must be sown as evenly as possible, and for this reason a calm day must be chosen, as a very slight wind will throw the seed into heaps. After sowing, the ground may be lightly harrowed if the surface is large, but if not, give it an even raking, but in either case the ground should be smoothed down with a roller or patted with a spade, so to form a smooth surface to be mowed. Although if a choice can be had, it is best to sow the lawn seed in early spring, yet it can be sown nearly as profitably in September, or in the more southerly states in October, or for that matter, even as late as May and June in spring, only if so late, it is better to mix one quart of oats to every bushel of grass-seed, that the oats may shade and protect the young grass from the sun until it has root enough to support itself. But if sown in March or April, or in September or October, there is no need of using the oats, as no injury will be done by the sun at these seasons. To keep the lawn in proper condition, it should be mowed over once every week if the weather is moist, and not less than once in two weeks, even in dry weather, for if the lawn has been properly made in the first place, and "top dressed" with a good coat of well-rotted manure in fall, and the rough raked off in spring, the weather must be dry and hot indeed to prevent its growth.

CHAPTER IX.

DESIGN FOR GARDEN.

As this book is intended to comprehend all the wants of a cottage or suburban garden, including flowers, fruits, and vegetables, it would increase its size too much to

2

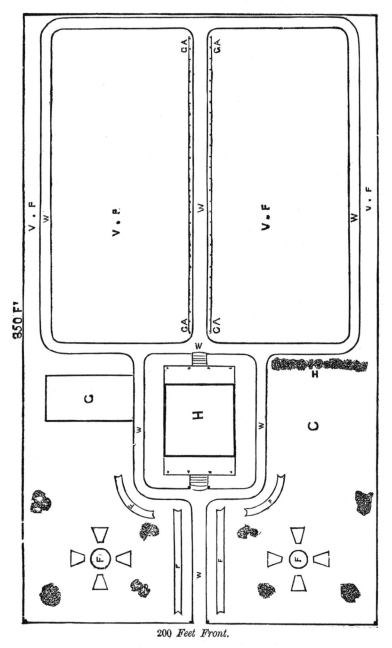

200 *Feet Front.*

Fig. 6.—DESIGN FOR LAYING OUT GROUNDS

give a great variety of designs for the flower-garden. To those that require such, some intelligent landscape gardener should be consulted. Intelligent, I say, for nine out of ten that pretend to be landscape gardeners are not ; but consult a man able to draw a neat design, for if he cannot do that he is not a very safe person to be intrusted with the working out of the plan of another. You are careful to ascertain that the architect for your house is a man of education and intelligence before you entrust yourself in his hands, but when it comes to designing the lawn and flower-grounds, the veriest bog-trotter, who styles himself a " landscaper," is too often allowed to display his " art," and at the same time make you ridiculous. Rest assured that if such a pretender has not had ambition enough to become fairly well instructed, he is not likely to show much taste in designing your grounds.

The design, (fig. 6), shows an area of 200 feet by 350, or a plot of nearly two acres, about one-third of the whole facing the street, is used for flower-garden and for dwelling, the two-thirds in the rear for fruit and vegetable grounds. There is a point in this sketch, to which I wish to call attention, as it is one too often lost sight of ; the flower-garden and lawn face the street, while the fruit and vegetable grounds are at the rear ; the view of these from the street is shut out upon one side by a screen or tall hedge of evergreens, H, and upon the other by a curvilinear glass structure, G, which may be used either as a grapery or a greenhouse. The walk, W, passes on each side of the house to connect with other walks at the rear ; the beds, F, may be planted in ribbon lines either with flowering plants or those with brilliant and strongly contrasting foliage. The flower-beds, F, each side of the entrance near the front, may be made of any form that may be preferred ; a simple circle planted as suggested in the next chapter, will produce a good effect, and be

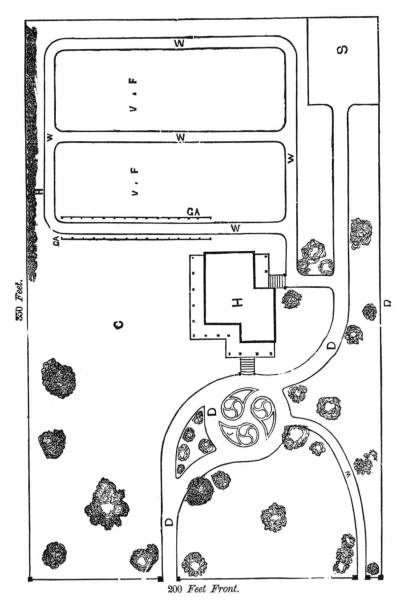

Fig. 7.—DESIGN FOR GROUNDS WITH CARRIAGE-DRIVE.

more easily cared for than beds of the style here given; most persons, where the floral ornamentation is, as in this case, confined to a few effective masses, prefer to change not only the manner of planting such beds each year, but to alter their form occasionally. The unbroken area of lawn at c is intended for a croquet ground. At the rear of the house the central walk is spanned by a grape arbor, G A, if one wishes the vines to afford shade, or a simple trellis may run each side; the borders next the fence on each side and at the rear, (not shown in the plan), may also be used for grapes, or will be convenient for raspberries, currants, and other small fruits. The large plots, V F, are for the main crops of vegetables and fruits; asparagus, rhubarb, strawberries, and such other crops as remain year after year without being disturbed, should be so placed at the outset as to be interfered with as little as possible in the frequent working of the soil necessary for other crops. A lot of this size will require the labor of one man, whose time must be exclusively devoted to the garden, and to nothing else, to keep it in proper order. Such is the extent, and something near the design of the grounds I use for such purposes. I generally have selected one of my most active men to take charge of it, and find he has plenty to do to do it well. A second design (fig. 7) shows a lot of the same dimensions, with a different arrangement, there being a stable, S, and no rear entrance, it is necessary to provide one from the front, and in order to secure a greater breadth of lawn, the house is placed at one side of the center of the grounds. The drive, D, in the design is made to turn around a group of flower-beds of fanciful pattern, but this may be replaced by a single circle, planted as suggested in the next chapter, or by a group of ornamental evergreen or other shrubs. In this design the croquet-ground is at c, and the grape arbor, G A, is used to shut out the view of the vegetable grounds from the street.

A row of closely planted evergreens at H serves to break the force of the winds ; the suggestions as to the other details in the preceding plan, (fig. 6), apply to this also.

———•◦•———

CHAPTER X.

PLANTING OF LAWNS AND FLOWER-BEDS.

The subject of lawn planting, including the proper setting and grouping of trees and shrubs, and their most effective disposal, is too extended for the scope of this book. These matters belong to works upon landscape gardening, and are ably treated in those by Downing, Kemp, Weidenmann, Scott, and others. But the planting of flower-beds comes properly within our limits. The old-fashioned mixed borders of four or six feet wide along the walks of the fruit or vegetable garden, were usually planted with hardy herbaceous plants, the tall growing at the back, with the lower growing sorts in front. These, when there was a good collection, gave a bloom of varied color throughout the entire growing season. But the more modern style of flower borders has quite displaced such collections, and they are now but little seen, unless in very old gardens, or in botanical collections. Then again, we have the mixed borders of bedding plants, a heterogeneous grouping of all kinds of tropical plants, still holding to the plan of either placing the highest at the back of the border if it has only one walk, or if a bed has a walk on each side, the highest in the middle, and the plants sloping down to the walk on each side. The mixed system still has its advocates, who deprecate the modern plan of massing in color as being too formal, and too unnatural a way to dispose of flowers. But be that as it may, we will not stop to argue the matter further than to state, that in a visit to England in 1872, it was most evident that the "Carpet Styles" of massing plants as done at Battersea Park, London, were interesting to the people in a way that no mixed border could ever be. Any one who has not yet seen the wonderful effects produced by the massing of plants in this way, has a treat before him. Nearly all the public parks in and about London are so planted, and thousands of cottage gardens vie with each other in imitation of the parks. But to plant in patterns or in ribbon lines requires for immediate effect a large number of plants, for the reason that they must be so set out that they will meet to form continuous masses shortly after planting.

An illustration in circles (for convenience), is given in fig. 8, to show what plants can be massed together to give a pleasing effect. Of course it will be understood that a bed of any shape can be planted in this manner as well as circular beds, only keeping in view the *width* of the bed. For example, a bed having a diameter of ten feet may require eight or ten different kinds of plants to form the necessary contrast, while that of five feet will not re-

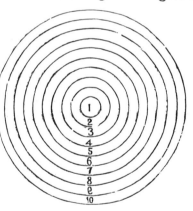

Fig. 8.—DIAGRAM OF FLOWER-BED.

quire more than half that number. The following named plants are well suited for planting in masses or ribbon lines ; they are named as nearly as possible in the order of their hight, number one in each case being the tallest. Many of them will require to be "pinched back" to keep at the proper hight, so that the outline will form a regular slope from the center or highest point, down to the front or lowest point—thus in list No. 1, Canna Indica zebrina will grow six feet high, while Lobelia Paxtoni,

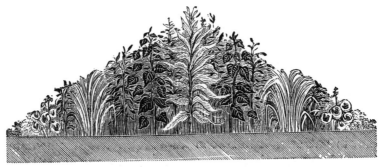

Fig. 9.—SECTION OF FLOWER-BED.

the lowest, is less than six inches. The section given in figure 9 will give an idea of the arrangement of a bed of this kind.

List No. 1.
Average hight in feet.

1. Canna Indica zebrina, leaves green and brown striped........6
2. Salvia splendens, flowers scarlet...........................5
3. Golden Coleus, leaves orange and brown.....................4
4. Achyranthes Lindeni, leaves rich crimson...................3
5. Phalaris arundinacea var., leaves white and green............2½
6. Achyranthes Gilsoni, leaves carmine........................2
7. Bronze Geranium, leaves golden bronze......................1½
8. Centaurea candida, leaves white............................1
9. Alternanthera latifolia, leaves crimson and yellow........... ¾
10. Lobelia Paxtoni, flowers blue.............................. ½

List No. 2.
Average hight in feet.

1. Caladium esculentum, leaves large green......................5
2. Japanese Maize, leaves striped white and yellow.............5
3. Coleus Verschaffeltii, leaves chocolate crimson..............4
4. Delphinium bicolor, flowers blue and white.................3
5. Cyperus alternifolius var., leaves white and green............2½
6. Achyranthes Verschaffeltii, leaves crimson...................2
7. Mountain of Snow Geranium, leaves white and green..........1½
8. Tropæolum, Ball of Fire, flowers flame color.................1
9. Echeveria metallica, leaves gray, metallic lustre.............. ¾
10. Alternanthera amœna, yellow and carmine.................... ½

It will be understood that these lists of plants can be transposed in any way necessary to suit beds of all widths, keeping in view that where small beds are placed near walks the lower growing kinds are most suitable, while for beds at greater distances from walks, or other points of view, the taller growing kinds must be used. Very fine effects are produced by planting on a lawn a single specimen of stately habit, such as some varieties of the Ricinus, or Castor-oil Bean, which grow ten and twelve feet in hight in one season, and are particularly striking plants. Or instead of this, a mass of six, eight, or twelve plants of scarlet sage will form a group six feet high by as many in diameter, and its dazzling scarlet color, contrasting against the green of the lawn, is superb. Many of the Amaranths are also well suited for planting in single groups. *Amarantus tricolor gigantea,* (Joseph's coat), grows to the hight of six feet, and its leaves in the late summer and fall months exceed in brilliancy of color anything we know of in foliage ; scarlet, crimson, and golden yellow predominating. Another, the *Amarantus bicolor ruber,* grows to the hight of five feet, and is plumed with scarlet crimson. In contrast to these, plants of a more somber tint may be used, in individual specimens or in a group of such as Pampas Grass, (*Gynerium argenteum*), or the Ravenna Grass, (*Erianthus Ravennœ*), each of these attain a hight from six to ten feet, and have a graceful appearance. The Tanyah, *Caladium esculentum,* a tropical looking plant growing three or four feet in hight, and producing leaves sometimes eighteen inches across.

THE CARPET STYLE OF FLOWER-BEDS.

Planting, as practised at Battersea and other parks in London, is as yet but little seen with us ; our public parks here have shown a lamentable want of taste in this matter, especially those of New York and Brooklyn ; Philadelphia and Boston have done better, but all of these are weak attempts when compared with the grounds of some of our private gentlemen, notable among whom are H. W. Sargent, of Peekskill, N. Y., and H. H. Hunnewell, of Boston. The grounds of Mr. H. are thrown open to the public, who have the opportunity of seeing effects in this style of planting, nearly equal to anything in Europe, entirely at the expense of the munificent owner. The carpet style, so called, consists in using plants that can be kept down to a few

Fig. 10.—DESIGN FOR SCROLL-PATTERN.

inches above the level of the lawn. A great variety of succulent plants are used, such as Echeverias, Sedums, Mesembryanthemums, etc., together with numerous low-growing Alpine plants, such as Ajugas, Cerastiums, Lysimachias, Lobelias, Ivies, Alternantheras, etc., etc. This style of bedding requires an immense number of plants. One bed in the carpet style at Battersea Park, containing less than 1,000 square feet, required 4,000 plants to produce the desired effect in the design, and not a leaf of these was more than six inches above the lawn. Planting in this style admits of unlimited variety in the form of the beds, and contrasts of colors ; so great is the care exercised abroad in arranging the designs that colored papers, giving the exact tints of the leading flowers and colored foliage, are supplied by the dealers, in order that colored designs may be made and

Fig. 11.—ORNAMENTAL DESIGN, AFTER THOMPSON.

studied before putting them into execution ; a single misplaced color may spoil the effect of the whole. In works of this kind the parts of the design should be separated by well defined portions of turf, as the color of each member of it is brought out more clearly and distinctly, and the whole has a much better effect if a liberal amount of green is introduced. The two plans, figs. 10 and 11, are introduced to give an idea of some of the

simpler designs; the scroll-work, fig. 10, in various forms
is much used, either near a drive, or as a margin or
frame to more elaborate work.

CHAPTER XI.

FALL, OR HOLLAND BULBS.

These bulbs are mainly such as are imported from Holland in the fall, and consist of Hyacinths, Tulips, Crocuses, Jonquils, Narcissuses, Snow-drops, and various
other less known kinds. With few exceptions, all these
bulbs are hardy in our most northern states, though all
are benefitted by a covering of two or three inches of
rough litter or leaves spread over the beds before freezing
weather. The soil best suited for all bulbs is a rich, but
rather sandy loam. All these bulbs may be planted any
time from the middle of September, until the ground is
closed by frost in December. Hyacinths should be
planted at distances of eight or ten inches apart each
way, and from three to four inches deep. Tulips, the
same distance apart, but a little less deep. Crocuses four
inches apart and two inches deep. Jonquils and Narcissuses may be planted six inches apart and four inches
deep. Snow-drops the same as Crocuses.

Very fine effects are produced by planting Hyacinths in
lines each of one color, or when mixed colors are placed
in the lines, care must be taken to have them arranged
so that the bed will give harmonious blending of color.
Crosuses have nearly the same range of color as the
Hyacinth, and may be planted either way.

All these bulbs are easily grown in pots. The Hyacinth requires a pot six inches in depth and diameter; in

potting it is only necessary to fill the pot rather loosely to the brim, and press the bulb down, so that only about one-fourth of it appears above the soil. The pot should then be struck smartly on the bench to give the soil the proper degree of firmness, leaving it, when finished, about an inch or so below the rim of the pot. Then water freely to still further settle the soil. The pots should then be placed where it is cool and dark, which will encourage a strong development of roots, before the bud starts to grow at the top. Such a situation can be made by covering up the pots with four or five inches of sand in a cool cellar, under the stage of a cool greenhouse, or in a sunken pit, in each case covering with sand or leaves, so as to exclude heat and frost, for it must not be forgotten that a strong development of root can only be had at a low temperature, say from forty to fifty degrees, and any attempt to force them to make roots quicker by placing them in a high temperature, will most certainly enfeeble the flower. If we will only observe how nature points out to us this necessity, we will see how safe it will be to follow her. In all hardy plants, the roots in spring, (when the temperature is low), form the rootlets before a leaf or flower is developed. To show the bad effects when this is not the case, take a root of any of our hardy lilies and plant it in March, and take a similar bulb and plant it in May; it will be found that the early planted bulb that had an opportunity to slowly develop its roots before there was heat enough to start the top, will give a finer growth and finer flower than the bulb that was planted in May, and run up into growth before it had an opportunity to sufficiently push its roots into the soil. The culture of all the bulbs before named, in pots, is the same as that of the Hyacinth, only the Narcissuses and Tulips should be planted three or four in a six or seven-inch pot, and Crocuses ten or twelve in a pot. All these bulbs may likewise be grown in moss, or even pure sand, provided that it is kept damp ; the necessity being a medium wherein the roots can revel in moisture.   But whether potted in soil, sand, or moss, there will be no need to water, but at the time of potting, provided the pots have been covered up as directed, and kept cool and dark.   If potted say the first week in October, they may be removed from their dark quarters in seven or eight weeks, only before doing so, turn a few of them out of the pots to see whether they have rooted around the ball of earth. They may then be placed in full light and watered freely.

HYACINTHS IN GLASSES.

Although the Jonquils and Narcissuses can be grown in water in glasses as well as the Hyacinth, they are not often so treated, hyacinths being the only bulbs largely flowered in that way, some of which are shown in fig. 12.

Belgian.   *Vase-shaped.*   *Bohemian.*

Fig. 12.—HYACINTH GLASSES.

The glasses are made of various styles, from the plain old-fashioned Belgian to the ornamental Bohemian glasses, and of clear glass or colored, green, amber, claret, and other shades.   The glasses, which are best of a dark color, are filled with water just high enough for the base of the bulb to touch it.   The glasses must be placed in a cool and dark place, just such a situation as recommended for those grown in pots. Care must be taken that they do not freeze, else the glasses will be broken, and the Hyacinths more or less injured. Single Hyacinths are better than double ones for glasses. The water should be changed every six or eight days.

---◦◦---

CHAPTER XII.

PROPAGATION OF PLANTS BY SEEDS.

Nature provides abundantly for the reproduction of plants, and the difficulty of multiplying by one method is compensated by the ease with which it may be done in another. Whenever we find a plant takes root with difficulty from " slips " or cuttings, in nine cases out of ten we find that it seeds freely, and gives us a ready means of increase. Thus we find the much admired Centaureas, one kind of the " Dusty Millers," the white leaved plants now so much used in massing and for baskets, are exceedingly difficult and slow to root from cuttings, but are readily raised from seeds. Our fine strains of blotched Petunias are also troublesome as cuttings, but make plants quickly from seeds. The Cyclamen with its turnip-like stem or bulb, could only be propagated by cutting in pieces, disfiguring its shape, and requiring years to form a circular bulb again, but here we have seed coming to our help which germinates freely, and makes a flowering plant in one year. The Apple Geranium never affords proper cuttings from which to make a plant, but it seeds freely, from which splendid plants can be produced in a few months. So the Primulas and Cinerarias, both slow and uncertain from cuttings, seed freely. Echeveria metallica, one of the beau-

tiful plants of the House-Leek family, produces no bud
from the base of the leaf, as nearly all the other species
do, but to make up, it seeds abundantly, and so with
hundreds of other plants to which our space will not permit us to refer. There is no rule by which we can des-
ignate what plants are best propagated by seeds, and
what by cuttings, experience being the only teacher, and
even the experience of a lifetime is too short for those
of us that have had the largest practice.

Seedling plants can be nearly as well raised in the window of a sitting-room or parlor, provided the temperature is right, as in a greenhouse, for seeds do not need a
strong direct light while germinating, in fact that is
often a difficulty in a greenhouse, as the surface of the
seed-bed dries up too quickly in the direct sunshine, ne-
cessitating watering, which bakes the surface. The best
thing wherein to sow seeds is shallow boxes; these need
not be more than two or three inches deep, with open
seams at the bottom through which water will drain
quickly. Fill the boxes within half an inch of the top
with light rich earth; if it can be procured, nothing is
better than black leaf-mold from the woods, or light
sandy soil mixed with an equal bulk of stable manure, so
rotted as to resemble leaf-mold, it will not answer unless rotted as fine as dust. In the absence of either of
these, sweepings from a paved street are excellent, mixed
with light sandy soil, the object in all cases being *light-
ness* of the soil or mold in which the seed is to be sown;
for if tiny seeds, as many of our flower-seeds are, are
embedded in a stiff soil, the germ in many of them is too
weak to push its way to the light. When the proper soil
has been secured, pat it down with a smooth board until
it is as smooth and level as it well can be, then sow the
seed carefully over the surface, distributing it evenly,
then take a common kitchen sieve and sift just so much
earth evenly over the seed as will cover it and no more:

then take a watering-pot with the finest kind of a rose, and shower the earth with the spray. Keep the box at a temperature as near sixty degrees as possible, taking care to give it a shower of spray only when the surface appears to be dry ; but few seeds will fail to germinate under such conditions. But after the seeds have "brairded," as the Scotch gardeners say, comes another difficulty ; in quite a number of plants, particularly if sown in the house, just as soon as the seed leaf has developed, and before the first rough or true leaves have formed, the seedling is attacked by a minute fungus, that will often sweep off the whole crop in 48 hours, if not attended to. The required attention is, that as soon as there are indications of the " damping off" of these tiny seedlings, they must be carefully taken up and planted out in similar boxes, prepared exactly as the seed-boxes have been ; they may be planted quite closely, not more than half an inch apart, and let their further treatment be exactly the same as in germinating the seeds. In the course of a few weeks they will have grown freely, and they may then be lifted and placed in similar boxes, but wider apart, say three or four inches, or potted singly in two and a half or three-inch pots as most convenient, until such a time as they are to be planted out in the open ground, or to be used otherwise. In this way as great a number of plants may be raised from a 25c. or 50c. packet of seed as would cost $25 or $50 to purchase, besides the far greater satisfaction of their being the products of your own hands.

CHAPTER XIII.

PROPAGATION OF PLANTS BY CUTTINGS.

There is no more interesting operation to the amateur gardener than that of increasing his stock of plants by cuttings or slips. Heretofore, it was accounted a great mystery, and unless with some of the commonest kinds of Geraniums, few amateurs ever presumed to invade the territory of the professional gardeners. Nearly all writers on the subject had so befogged this simple matter with technical nonsense, that few, not regularly brought up to the business, presumed to attempt it. We now consider it one of our simplest operations, far simpler than raising many kinds of plants from seed, and though we raise now over two millions of plants annually, and keep a man with three assistants doing nothing else the entire year but propagating plants from slips, yet we could take any careful, intelligent man from among our garden laborers, and install him as a competent propagator in a month. Where plants are propagated from cuttings in large numbers, we elevate a bench, usually four feet wide, above the flue or hot-water pipes, to within a foot or so of the glass at the front, and on this table or bench we place three or four inches of sand, of any color or texture, provided it is not from the sea-shore, and contains salt. This bench is boarded down in front, so as to confine the heat from the flue or pipes under it, and give what is called "bottom heat"; the sand on a bench so formed will indicate a temperature of perhaps seventy degrees, while the atmosphere of the greenhouse, particularly during the night, will be ten degrees less. Now, if the cuttings are in the right condition, and are inserted an inch or so in this sand, freely watered, and shaded from the sun from 9 or 10 A.M. to 3 or 4 P.M., cuttings of nearly all kinds of plants are certain to take root in from ten to twenty days.   But the cuttings must be in the right condition, and this is best shown by the engraving, (fig. 13).   It will be observed that the upper portion of the shoot is snapped or broken, while the other is only kneed or bent ; this snapping point, as we now term it, is a true indication of proper condition of the cutting ; where it bends and does not break, it is too hard, and though a

Fig. 13.—PROPER AND IMPROPER STATE OF CUTTING.

cutting will root, when in that condition, it will be slower in doing so, and the roots thrown out from it will be weaker and more wiry than when emitted from a cutting taken in the condition in which it breaks.   Besides the plant grown from the older cutting will not likely be so healthy or vigorous as one made when the shoot is in the proper state.

In propagating woody plants, such as Roses, Azaleas, or Camellias, this test of breaking or snapping of the cutting does not in these indicate the proper condition, although they also will root if taken in the soft state, yet we find it is not quite so well to do so as to wait until the cuttings of these woody plants gets harder ; what this proper hardness is, it is not very easy always to determine. In roses the best condition for taking the cutting is reached when the young shoot, (of which the cutting is made), develops the flower bud to about the size of a large pea. Although the shoot on which the flower bud shows, will make a proper enough cutting, yet if it is not desired to waste the flower, cuttings had better be made of the "blind" shoots, *i. e.*, such young shoots as do not flower. In making the cuttings of roses, or in fact of almost all plants, (with a few exceptions hardly worth noting), there is no need to cut at a joint, although nine gardeners out of ten still do so, particularly those who have learned the business in Europe, where, in this as in many other things in horticulture, they still follow the dictum of some savant of a century ago, never questioning why. But our business necessities here, have caused us to ride rough-shod over many of their set rules, and in none more ruthlessly than in this matter of propagating. But as this book is written mainly for amateurs in gardening, I will proceed to give a simple method by which any one can propagate plants from cuttings or slips, even when no greenhouse or hot-bed is at hand. It is called

THE "MUD" OR "SAUCER SYSTEM" OF PROPAGATING.

Take any common saucer or plate, into which put sand to the depth of an inch or so, then prepare the cuttings in the usual manner, and insert them in the sand close enough to touch each other as in fig. 14. The sand is then to be watered to bring it to the condition of mud. The saucer with the cuttings is then placed on the shelf of the greenhouse, in the hot-bed, or in a sunny window of any room in the dwelling house ; in each case fully exposed to the sun and never shaded. But one condition is essential to success—until the cuttings become rooted, *the sand must be kept continually saturated with water and always in the condition of mud.* To do this the saucers must be watered at least once a day with a very fine rose watering pot, and the watering must be done very gently, else the cuttings may be washed out. There is every probability that ninety per cent of all cuttings put in will take root, provided they were in the proper condition, and the temperature has not been lower than 65 degrees nor above 100 degrees. By the saucer system a higher temperature may be main-

Fig. 14.—SAUCER PROPAGATION.

tained without injury, as the cuttings are in reality placed in water, and will not wilt provided the water is not allowed to dry up. Still the detached slip, until rooted, will not endure a long continuation of 100 degrees, and we advise that propagation be done at such seasons that the cuttings, wherever they may be, will have as near as possible an average temperature of 75° or 80° *in the sunlight.* The cuttings will root (according to kinds and the temperature), in from six to twenty days. Verbenas, Heliotropes, Fuchsias, etc., root in a week, while Roses, Carnations, or Azaleas, take two, three, or four weeks. When rooted they should be potted in light soil, (such as recommended in the article "Propagating of Plants by Seeds,") in pots from two to three inches in diameter, and treated carefully by shading and watering for two or three days. To such as desire more extended information on the subject of propagating plants by cuttings, I would refer to my work, "Practical Floriculture."

CHAPTER XIV.

PROPAGATING BY LAYERING.

Although florists now rarely resort to propagation by layering, yet now and then it may be desirable for amateurs to increase the number of some favorite plant during the summer season, where no other method of propagation can be practised. The only difference between a layer and a cutting is, that the cutting is entirely detached from the parent plant, while the layer remains partially connected with it. Although layering may be done with the ripened wood of vines or shrubs of the growth of the previous season, yet it is preferable to use the shoot of the present year in its half green state ; for example, a rose or flowering shrub is pruned in the usual way in spring; by midsummer it will have made strong shoots one, two, or three feet in length from or near the base of the plant. Take the shoot then in the left hand, (after having stripped it of its leaves for a few inches on each side of where it is to be cut), keep the fingers under the shoot, and make a cut on the *upper part,*

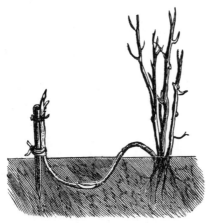

Fig. 15.—PROPAGATING BY LAYERING.

an inch or so in length, and to about half the thickness of the shoot, then slightly twist the " tongue" or cut part to one side, as shown in the engraving, fig. 15; having opened a shallow trench, fasten the branch down with a hooked peg, and cover with earth ; it is a good plan to place a flat stone over the layer to prevent the soil from drying out. This plan of cutting the shoot in layering is rarely shown in illustrations on the subject, the cuts usually being represented at the under side of the shoot. When cut at the lower side, the shoot can not be laid down without danger of breaking it.

CHAPTER XV.

ABOUT GRAFTING AND BUDDING.

It is often desirable to be able to bud or graft one variety of plant on another entirely different variety ; and it is an interesting fact to know that the bud taken from one plant and inserted so that it grows in another, and is entirely sustained by the plant into which it has been budded, in no way changes its character. This fact is so well known to gardeners that they rarely think it necessary to mention it in writing on the subject, and many amateurs interested in horticultural matters have very confused notions on budding. To illustrate: if a leaf bud is taken from a white Rose, and inserted in the stem of a red Rose, all the branches that proceed from this bud, leaves or flowers, will be identical with the white Rose from which it was taken. Or if a leaf bud of the red Rose be inserted in the white, the same result would follow; it will be identical in all respects with the red variety. Or you may take a bud or graft from the sourest crab apple, and insert it into a branch of the sweetest apple tree you can find, and the shoot which grows from the crab apple bud will ever remain a crab, and will in no way be affected by the sweet apple stock on which it is growing. Or if the operation is reversed, and the sweet apple is budded or grafted on the sour, the result will be the same ; its individuality will be in no way changed, it will be identical with the variety from which it was taken.

Still further to illustrate this matter of budding or grafting, you may take a rose-bush having any number of shoots, it makes no difference whether one or a hundred ; on each shoot you may bud a distinct variety of Rose, of all the colors, forms or odors embraced in the Roses, and each one will hold its distinct characteristic of color, form, or fragrance, be it crimson, white, pink, or yellow in color, double or single in form, or of tea or other odor. Or you may take a young seedling apple tree, insert a bud of another into it, then after that bud has made a growth, bud still another variety into that, and so on as many as is desired, rub of all shoots in the stem that start below, and the variety last budded will hold its individuality unchanged, no matter though the life-sustaining sap flows through the cells of several different kinds. You may mark the space occupied by each of the varieties, and cut back to any particular variety, and the fruit that will be produced by that part, which will then be the top, will hold its character without change. What is true of roses and apples, is of course equally true of whatever plant that can be grafted or budded.

The stock does not in any manner affect the individuality of the graft, and I supposed that this was one of the generally accepted axioms of horticulture, but in a conversation not long ago with a gentleman whose opinion is entitled to consideration, I found him inclined to believe that there were some few exceptions to what was admitted to be a general law, and in support of his argument, he referred me for exceptions to Darwin's "Plants and Animals under Domestication." I have examined this work, and find only two cases wherein it is claimed that the graft is influenced by the stock, or the stock by the graft. The first is at page 457, Vol. 1, where "Prof. Caspary describes the case of a six-year-old white Moss Rose, which sent up several suckers, one of which was thorny and destitute of moss, exactly like those of the Provence Rose, (*R. centifolia*), another shoot bore both kinds of flowers, and in addition longitudinally striped flowers. As this white moss had been grafted on the Provence Rose, Prof. Caspary attributes the above changes to the influence of the stock, but from the facts already given, and from others to be given, bud variation with reversion is probably sufficient explanation"; and Darwin proceeds to give nearly a dozen cases of like variation where there was no grafting at all. A very marked case of this "bud variation" is at the present time existing in my own greenhouses. In a bed of about one hundred plants of the new tea-rose, "La Nankin," all made from the cuttings from one parent plant, we have had four distinct varieties. The original flower or bud has its base or lower half of a nankeen yellow color, while its upper half is pure white, the separate colors being clearly defined, yet among our plants from cuttings we have some flowers that are entirely of the nankeen color, without white; then again pure white with no nankeen, and on one shoot the flowers came of a light pink or blush shade. Now had Prof. Caspary a grafted plant of "La Nankin" playing these freaks, he no doubt would have concluded that it was the influence of the graft on the stock. There are other instances in grafting where an amalgamation of individualities *apparently* occurs; these cases are familiar to all horticulturists of much experience, and are also alluded to by Darwin in the work above

3

referred to. He gives a number of instances where the variegated Oleander grafted on the plain leaved variety as a
stock, imparts the variegation to the stock, or where a yel-
low-leaved ash tree, grafted on the common green-leaved
variety, produced a blotched or variegated variety. That
most of the variegation in the foliage of plants, is due to
disease, or at least some disturbance of the regular func-
tions of the leaf, there is but little doubt, and it is therefore but an accidental condition of the individual. Where
a variegated plant is budded or grafted upon a healthy
subject, the disease is transmitted from the unhealthy
bud or graft to the healthy stock in a manner somewhat
analogous to innoculation of smallpox virus in man. The
character or constitution of the individual is in no way
affected in the one case more than in the other. Marked
instances in which plain-leaved plants become variegated
by being grafted with variegated cions, are afforded by
the variegated Abutilons ; but in all such cases it is simply the "blotching" or "disease" of the foliage that
occurs, there is no change whatever in the coloring of the
flowers or shape of the leaves, the individuality of these
remains unchanged. That leaf variegation is indicative
of disease, is manifest from another fact. It is quite a
common thing to find a shoot sent out by the silver-
leaved or variegated Geraniums that is pure white in stem
and leaves, not a particle of green, or such golden variegated kinds of Geraniums as "Mrs. Pollock" will send
out a pure yellow shoot ; but all efforts to make plants of
such shoots will fail ; they may feebly root as cuttings,
or they may be grafted on a green-leaved, healthy stock
long enough to drag out a few weeks of existence, but the
disease is here thoroughly established, and all attempts
to propagate these entirely abnormal growths completely
fail. It has been claimed that the Duchesse d'Angouleme
and other pears are much better flavored when grafted on
the quince than on the pear stock, and these are quoted

as examples of the influence of the stock on the graft, but to me this seems capable of another explanation :

We know that the pear stock is a vigorous and rampant grower as compared with the quince, and may it not be that this vigor of growth in the tree impairs the flavor of the fruit in some varieties, just as we find the flavor of fruits impaired when grown in too rich soil ? The effect of soil upon quality is particularly marked in melons. I remember that I once grew a field of three acres of nutmeg melons, one-half of the patch was rich bottom land, and the other portion was a rather poor hillside. The fruit produced on the bottom was much larger, but so different from and inferior in flavor to those on the hillside that no one would have recognized the two as being of the same variety. The same, though in a less marked degree, probably occurs in other fruits under similar conditions. From these reasons I believe it safe to assert that no evidence has yet been shown wherein the stock in any manner affects the graft other than that it may cause it to grow stronger or weaker, just as the stock is strong or weak, and the amount of such influence will be only such as a rich or poor soil would produce. In other words, the " stock " is only a medium or soil wherein the grafted individual grows, and affects it no more than if it drew its sustenance direct from the earth—strong, if on a strong stock, as on a fertile soil, and weak, if on a weak stock, as on a sterile soil.

CHAPTER XVI.

HOW GRAFTING AND BUDDING ARE DONE.

After this discussion of general principles, let us come to the practice of grafting and budding. In what has been said, they have been used as synonyms, and their object is precisely the same—to propagate a particular plant upon a rooted plant of another kind. Among fruits we do this because we cannot multiply choice varieties by seed or by cuttings ; stocks are raised from seed, which if allowed to grow and bear, might produce a poor and worthless fruit, or it may be a good kind. To make matters sure, we graft a twig of a kind that we know upon a seedling about which we know nothing. With Camellias, the choice kinds cannot well be propagated from cuttings, but some of the commoner kinds will grow in this way, and the choice Camellias are grafted upon stocks obtained by rooting cuttings of the others ; so in various cases among fruits and flowers, budding or grafting affords the readiest, if not the only method, by which we can multiply certain varieties. A graft is a twig containing one or more buds, and so inserted or planted in the stock that the new bark and new wood of the two shall be in close contact ; in budding, a single bud with no wood, or as little wood as possible, is inserted or planted below the bark of the stock and in direct contact with its new or sap-wood. While we give the two operations different names, the French call budding simply a variety of grafting—shield-grafting. In a general way it may be stated that in grafting we use buds of a previous year, and insert them upon the stock where they are to grow the spring after they are formed, and as soon as vegetation starts, these buds commence to grow. In budding we use buds of the current season's growth ; the recently formed buds, near the end of the growing season, are planted in the stock where they unite, and remain dormant until spring, when the inserted bud pushes into growth at the time that the natural buds of the stock start. These statements apply only to out-door grafting and budding ; when these operations are performed under glass, the propagator has control of atmospheric conditions, and varies them to suit the subjects in hand. In

out-door grafting, such as that upon fruit-trees, the cions
are best if cut in the fall and preserved in sand or sawdust in the cellar during the winter; though with very
hardy sorts this is not essential, they should be cut before
any swelling of the buds takes place. The operation succeeds best when the buds on the cion are perfectly dormant, and those on the stock have swollen and about to
open.

GRAFTING.

The various methods of grafting are too many to describe
here; the simplest is the cleft graft; the stock is sawed
off and the end cleft or split for a few inches down
through the center, (fig. 16); the cion, (or two if the
stock is over an inch in
diameter), with two or three
buds, has its lower end
smoothly cut to form a
wedge a trifle thicker on
one side than the other,
(fig. 17); the cleft in the
stock is pried open by means
of an iron wedge or a wedge-
shaped stick, and the cion
or cions set with the thicker
edge of the wedge outward,
observing to bring the inner bark and new wood
of stock and cion in as

Fig. 16.   Fig. 17.   Fig. 18.
CLEFT GRAFTING.

close contact as possible; the opening wedge being
withdrawn, the spring of the stock will hold the cions
in place, (fig. 18); the junction is to be covered with
grafting wax, or waxed cloth, taking care to completely
cover every wounded portion of both stock and cion. It
is by this method that most of the grafting is done all
over the country; it is rude but very successful; the ob-

jection to it is that it leaves too great a wound to be
closed over.   For small stocks the whip-graft is generally
used ; it is much easier to do it than to describe it ; stock
and cion should be as near of a size as possible ; both are
cut with a similar slope, and in each slope is cut a tongue
as in fig. 19 ; when the two slopes are put together, the

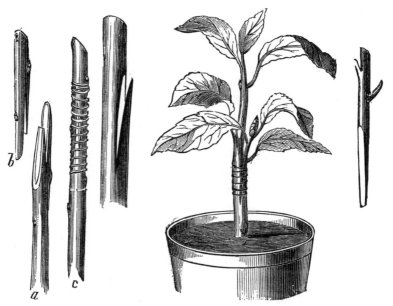

Fig. 19.—WHIP GRAFT.   Fig. 20.—SIDE GRAFT.

two tongues are interlocked as in the engraving, taking
care that the inner bark of stock and cion come in contact as completely as possible.   In this illustration the
parts are represented as tied with twine, to show the
joint below, but in practice the whole is completely covered with a band of waxed cloth.   This, where practicable, is an excellent graft, there being no large wounds to
heal over, and the points of union are numerous.   This
graft is much used by nurserymen in root-grafting small
apple and pear stocks.   A very simple form called the side-
graft is often employed by florists and nurserymen ; the

cion is cut to a long wedge, and the stock has a downward cut made in its stem into which the cion is inserted as in fig. 20. In grafting the Camellia and other hard-wooded plants, a combination of the whip and side graft is made use of as shown in fig. 21.

Grafting wax used to cover the wounds made in grafting may be purchased at the seed and implement stores, or the amateur can make it himself. It should be soft

Fig. 21.—GRAFTING THE CAMELLIA.

enough to be molded by the heat of the hand on a cool day, but not so soft as to run when exposed to the heat of the sun. It is essentially rosin and beeswax, with tallow or linseed oil enough to make it sufficiently soft. A good formula is rosin 2 lbs., beeswax $1^1|_4$ lb., tallow $^3|_4$ lb. The better way for the amateur to use this is to melt the whole together thoroughly and then dip in it strips of well worn cloth, such as may be torn from a worn-out sheet or calico dress. These waxed strips will tear readily, and may be neatly fitted to the graft to make a complete covering; the fingers should be slightly greased when applying the waxed cloth.

BUDDING

The shoot or stock to be budded upon must be in a thrifty growing state, so that the bark can be raised freely from the wood, and the bud to be inserted must be in such a state that it shows prominently at the axil of the leaf. Select a smooth portion of the stem of the stock, strip it of leaves, sufficiently to allow room for the operation, then make a cut through the bark to the wood of an inch or so, with a cross cut at the top, as shown in fig. 23; it will be observed that the illustration shows that a slight cut of the bark is made above the cross cut, this is done to allow the bud to slip in better; this custom we think is not general, but we find the operation is done quicker and better by its use.

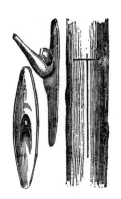  

Fig. 22.   Fig. 23.   Fig. 24.   Fig. 25.
BUD.   CUT.   BUD IN.   BUD TIED.

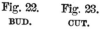

THE METHOD OF BUDDING.

Then take the shoot from which the bud is to be cut, and selecting a properly developed bud, cut it from the shoot as shown in fig. 22; if the portion of the shoot from which the bud is taken is well ripened, it is best to separate the wood from the bark of the bud; but if not it had better remain on. Usually it is necessary to take the wood from buds on the lower part of the shoot, while the upper part being less ripened, those buds may be inserted with the wood remaining. The edges of the cut in the

stock are lifted by the point of the knife or an ivory at-
tachment to the budding-knife, the bud inserted and
pushed down as in fig. 24; the portion of bark attached
to the bud that projects above the horizontal cut in the
stock is cut off, and the tie applied.   This is usually bast
matting, though cotton wick or other soft material will
do.   The engraving, fig. 25, shows where to place the
tie, but when of bast it quite covers the wound and excludes water and prevents drying.   In two or three weeks
after the bud has been inserted, it will be safe to remove
the tying, and if the operation has been performed on a
Rose in June, it will often make a considerable growth the
same season, but it usually lies dormant until the next
spring.   All shoots upon the stock below the bud must
be rubbed off, and when the bud that has been inserted
starts to grow, the stem above it must also be cut back
just above, so that the inserted bud which now becomes
the plant, may get the full benefit of the root.

CHAPTER XVII.

TREATMENT OF TROPICAL BULBS, SEEDS, ETC.

Any information that can be given in an article short
enough to be suitable for amateurs on a subject so extended as this must be confined to a few well known and
leading plants most valued for general cultivation.   First
may be placed the Tuberose, which in most northern
states must be artificially forwarded to bloom in perfection in the open air.   The seasons are too short for the
full development of the flowers in fall unless the bulbs
are so forwarded.   All that it is necessary to do is to
place the dry bulbs in soil in pots or in boxes about May

1st, (not before), keeping them rather dry until they
start to grow freely, when more water may be given.
Plant the bulbs thus started in the open border, the first
week in June.   The bulbs while being forwarded may be
kept in any place where the thermometer ranges from
about 65° to 75° at night.   We usually place them under or alongside the hot-water pipes in our greenhouses,
covering them up with paper to keep the heat of the
pipes from them.   Light is not necessary until they have
well started to grow.   A greenhouse is not essential for
starting them in, as a hot-bed, or even a warm sitting
room, will do nearly as well.   Any one wishing to have
their Tuberoses "started" can do it themselves just as
well as a florist can, and as the dry bulb costs less than
half the price of the started one, and is more safely
transported by mail or otherwise, any one taking the
trouble to do it will save expense and have the bulbs in
better condition for planting.

Some of my readers have seen or cultivated the bulbs
known as fancy or spotted-leaved Caladiums.   There are
probably no plants that assume such varied and wonderful markings of the leaves as these, and when properly
grown, they are among the most attractive plants at our
horticultural fairs.   The continued high temperature
necessary for the healthy growth of the Tuberose, is
equally indispensable for the Caladium.   The bulbs we
treat at first exactly in the same manner as the Tuberose; that is, they should not be started much before
May 1st, and never should they be kept for any length of
time in a less temperature than 65°.   They are best
started in small pots, and should be shifted into larger
ones as soon as these get filled with roots.   Started in
May, and properly treated, they should be large enough
by August or September to require a flower-pot twelve
inches in diameter, and the plant should be, according to
the variety, from two to three feet in diameter across the

leaves. Caladiums require a partial shade, and if kept in a greenhouse during summer, the glass should be shaded, but the light of an ordinary sitting-room would be just about right; so that even those who have not a greenhouse can grow these rather rare and beautiful plants with perfect ease. The only thing necessary if grown as a window plant, is to turn the pot around every few days so that each side may get a proper amount of light—a necessity with all plants grown in windows. The soil best suited for its growth is that known as sandy loam, to which should be added one-third rotted manure or leaf mold.

The same time of starting and a similarly high temperature is required for Begonias of all kinds, Bouvardias, Cissus, Coleuses, Dracænas, Euphorbias, Poinsettias, and all other plants known as "hot-house" or "tropical," and the same general treatment will in nearly all cases lead to satisfactory results. All of the plants or bulbs referred to will dwindle or die if long kept in a low temperature, and hence it is important that amateurs should remember that they ought not to attempt the cultivation of these plants unless they have the means of steadily keeping up the necessary high temperature. For that reason we recommend that they should not be started before May, as then they run less risk of being chilled.

What is true of tropical bulbs or plants is equally so of tropical seeds. Those who have not had experience or who have not the means of keeping up the necessary high temperature, should not sow the seeds of tropical plants before April 1st. Of vegetable seeds, the best known of this class are the Tomato, Pepper, and Egg-plant. I know they are often started in March in hot-beds or greenhouses with satisfactory results, but let any one try the experiment of sowing on March 1st and on April 1st, and note the result in the earliness of the crops, from the two sowings, and he will find that the chances are that the last shall be first ; if it were always practicable to keep the necessary temperature steadily along, the first sown would be the first, but this is often very difficult to accomplish, while there is but little difficulty with the later sowing, as assistance is then given by the increasing outside temperature.   For this reason seeds of tropical annual flowers, such as Amaranths of all kinds, Balsams, Salvias, Double Portulacas, Cannas, Coxcombs, Zinnias, etc., should not be sown before April in the hot-bed, or if in the open ground, in this latitude, not before May 15th.

CHAPTER XVIII.

THE POTTING OF PLANTS.

This naturally follows the preceding chapter, and I will briefly state a few of the most important points ; first of all is soil, or potting mold, often rather a troublesome thing to get by those who have only a few dozen plants to repot.   The soil used by us, and most florists, for nearly every plant we grow, is one combining freshness, richness, and what is called friableness of texture ; this condition we get by paring off the sod from the roadside, mixing it with one-third of well-rotted stable manure, and throwing it in heaps until it rots ; turning it over two or three times until the whole is well mixed ; if the plants are small, we run it through a fine sieve before using it ; if large, we use it rough, without sifting.   But it may not always be convenient to get this material, and it is by no means indispensable to success ; leaf-mold from the woods, mixed with any fresh field loam, and a little rotted stable manure, will answer nearly as well ;

or city folks can get sweepings from the pavements, and these mixed in equal bulk with any good fresh soil, that from an old cultivated garden is not usually so good, will make a potting soil in which almost any plant will grow vigorously ; of late years we have used street sweepings largely in our potting soil, and like it very much.

Now having the soil in proper condition, the next thing is the pots, which, if they are not new, should be thoroughly washed, so that the evaporation of moisture will take place freely through the porous sides. One of the most common errors among amateur cultivators is to put their plants in too large pots. If a plant such as a Rose or Geranium is lifted up out of the ground to be potted, it should be placed in a pot only large enough to allow an inch or so of soil to be placed below, and around its roots,—or to make it better understood, if the plants are, say a foot high, and a foot in diameter, they should be pruned back so that the diameter will not be more than 6 or 8 inches, and for such sized plants the pot should not be more than 6 inches wide and deep.

The same rule applies to plants that have been growing in pots; if it is now in a pot three inches wide, a proper shift will be to one four or four and a half inches wide ; if in a five-inch, shift to six and a half or seven-inch, and so on. In taking a plant out of a pot to place it in another one, turn it upside down with the fingers of the left hand spread over the surface of the earth, or top of the ball ; with the right hand holding the pot by the bottom, give the rim a smart rap on the edge of a board, and the ball of earth enveloping the root will come out, just as a jelly will out of a mold. I am particular in referring to this simple matter, knowing that it is no uncommon thing for ladies to break the pot with a hammer in their endeavors to get at the root, although they would hardly sacrifice a bowl to get at the jelly. In shifting, or repotting, place a little soil in the bottom of the pot, then place in the ball of roots exactly in the center, which will leave a space of from half an inch to two or three inches between this and the sides of the pot, according to the size of plant to be shifted; to pack this space between the side of the pot and the ball of roots with soil, it is better to use a flat stick with which to crowd it in moderately firm, filling up the pot to within an inch or so of the rim, this space being required to enable it to hold water. After potting, give a good watering with a sprinkler to settle the soil to the bottom of the pot, but after this be sparing of water until the plant shows signs of new growth, which will take place simultaneously with its making roots in the fresh soil. We use no potsherds or drainage of any sort in our pots, believing it to be perfectly useless to do so, the evaporation from the porous sides of the pot in our dry climate giving drainage enough. In the greenhouse we always spread an inch or so of sand on the bench or table upon which the plants stand; this to some extent prevents the plants from being injured when watering has been too long neglected, as the pots and the soil imbibe moisture from the sand which is usually more or less wet. When the plants are placed on bare shelves, either in the sitting-room where they are well exposed to light, or in the greenhouse, watering should be done at least once a day, provided they are growing vigorously.

CHAPTER XIX.

WINTER FLOWERING PLANTS.

The increase in the taste for winter-flowering plants, within the past five years, has been even more positive than that for the cultivation of plants out of doors, formerly it was rare for florists to fill an order in the fall, but now, during the months of October, November, and December, they make shipments daily in large quantities to every section of the country ; and these nearly equaling in number those of plants for the open ground in May and June. The plants best suited for flowering in winter may be divided into two classes. First, those requiring a moderate temperature at night, say an average of 50 degrees. Whether the plants are grown in the parlor or sitting-room of a private dwelling, or in a greenhouse especially constructed for their culture, the conditions should be as nearly as possible the same ; that is, uniformity of temperature ranging from 45° to 55°, and an avoidance of a dry atmosphere ; it is easy enough in the greenhouse to get a properly humid atmosphere by sprinkling the paths with water ; but in a room in the dwelling house, the only thing that can be done is to place pans of water on the stove, furnace, or whatever may be the source of heat. If plants are kept in a sitting-room or parlor, an east, south-east, or south aspect should be chosen. Plants of the class that may be grown at an average temperature of 50 degrees, are Azaleas, Abutilons, Ageratums, Carnations, Cinerarias, Catalonian Jessamines, Cape Jessamines, Camellias, Callas, Chorizemas, Geraniums of all kinds, Hibiscus, Hyacinths, Myrsiphyllum, (Smilax), Mahernias, Primulas, Stevias, Roses, Violets, and the various kinds known as *greenhouse* plants, which, together with those above named, can be found fully described in the florists' catalogues.

The second class, or hot-house plants, require an average temperature of 60 degrees at night, the range of which, however, may occasionally run from 55° to 65° without injury. Of these we name the following : Begonias, Bouvardias, Clerodendrons, Euphorbias, Epiphyllums, Fuchsias, Heliotropes, Poinsettia, Roses, (these will do in either temperature), Tuberoses, etc. For de-

scriptions of varieties, reference may be made to the catalogues.   The necessity for this difference in temperature
is not absolute, as many plants will do partially well in
either ; but we make this distinction as a guide to those
having a choice of temperatures, in order that they may
select the plants that are best adapted to the one at command.   In a greenhouse, particularly if heated by a flue,
there is often a difference of five or ten degrees between
one end and the other ; in such a case the plants named
in the first class must be placed at the cool end, and those
of the second class at the other.

One of the most troublesome pests of plants grown in
the greenhouse, or sitting-room, in winter, is the aphis,
or " green fly," as it is termed; we have no difficulty in
getting rid of it in the greenhouse, when it is separate
from the house ; all that is necessary is to get some tobacco stems (such as are thrown out as refuse by cigar
makers), and soak them in water for a minute or two ;
about half a pound or so for a greenhouse 25 x 20 feet is
placed over a small handful of shavings, only enough to
light the dampened tobacco, as too many might injure
the plants by smoke ; the burned tobacco stems give out
a smoke that is quickly fatal to the " green fly."   To
thoroughly prevent the least appearance of this insect, the
greenhouse must be fumigated every four or five days.
We fumigate all our greenhouses twice each week during
the entire year ; our rule being that an aphis must never
be seen upon any plant in the houses.   If the greenhouse
is attached to the dwelling, so that the tobacco smoke
would find its way into the rooms, recourse may be had
to another remedy ; take these same waste tobacco stems
and steep them in water until the liquid is of the color
of strong tea, with this water syringe the plants freely
twice a week, this will not only effectually destroy the
green fly, but will keep in check most other insects that
infest plants.   Where only a few plants are kept in

rooms, the easiest way is to dip the plants entirely in the tobacco water, moving them up and down in the liquid, to wash the insects off if they have a firm hold. The "red spider" is another pest to winter blooming plants, and wherever it is seen you may be certain that the atmosphere has been too dry, and very likely the temperature too hot, as it is rarely found in a cool, damp atmosphere. The treatment for this insect in the greenhouse is copious syringings with water, but where but a few plants are grown in the house, it is best to go over the leaves, especially on the under side, with a wet sponge. The red spider is so minute that it is hardly distinguishable by the naked eye, but its destructive effects are quickly perceivable, as the leaves upon which it works soon become brown, and if the leaves are closely examined, particularly the underside, the minute insect will be seen in great numbers.

Another troublesome insect among plants that are grown in a high temperature is the "mealy bug." The insect is flat, of whitish brown, usually nestling at the axils of the leaves, where it is covered with a white powder, making it easily distinguishable ; this is one of the most annoying of all insects that attack plants, as nothing seems to kill it, unless the remedy is strong enough to injure the plants ; so that rubbing it off with a small brush is the only safe remedy that we would care to recommend to amateurs. We find alcohol thrown on by what is called an "atomizer," sold by druggists for bedewing with perfumes, to be very effective in destroying the "mealy bug," as the alcohol reaches to every part of the plant, but we also find that some plants when in very soft growth are injured by even this light application of alcohol. Another pest, not an insect, but a vegetable parasitic growth known as mildew, affects but few plants in-doors except the rose, still as it is most injurious to those, we give the most effectual remedy for destroying mildew on roses either outside or under cover. Boil one lb. of lime and one lb. of sulphur in two gallons of water, until it is reduced to one gallon ; allow the liquid to settle until clear, and bottle it for use ; one gill only, no more, of this liquid, is mixed in five gallons of water, and this syringed thoroughly over the rose plants in the evening. If in the house, so that syringing cannot be done, dip the plants in it as recommended for the tobacco water. As with most other remedies, we prefer to use this lime and sulphur mixture as a preventive rather than as a cure, and we apply it to our roses at least once a week, even though there is no appearance of mildew. In proportion as plants are kept free from insects and mildew, so will be their vigor and their thriftiness. For more complete information see special chapter on insects and mildew.

I may here warn the amateur against the too common practice of placing plants in too large pots. As a general thing, when plants are received from the florists, they are sent without pots, and are usually in a condition requiring them to be shifted into a pot larger than they had been growing in; for example, if they have been grown in a pot of 3 inches diameter, place them in one a size larger, or 4 inches in diameter ; if they were in 4-inch pots give them one 5 or 6 inches across, and so on. Though we entirely ignore the use of crocks, or drainage in pots in our own practice, where we have always the proper sizes to use in potting, yet in cases where a suitable sized pot is not on hand into which to shift, (for example, if a plant that has been grown in a pot of 3 inches diameter, must be put in one of 6 inches), then by all means fill up one-third of this too large pot with broken pots, charcoal, or some such material to drain off the surplus moisture that would otherwise be injurious, in consequence of the pot being too large for the plant ; but if the pot into which it is, shifted is properly adjusted to the wants of the plant, the putting in of crocks for drainage is worse than useless, I care not what the plant may be. Our greenhouse establishment now covers nearly two acres, yet not a pot is so "drained." The need of a larger pot is shown by the earth becoming so filled with roots that they well cover the outside of the ball, but shifting into a larger pot should be done while the roots are yet white; if left until the roots get thoroughly matted, brown, and hard, it is too late, and the future growth will be seriously retarded. If the plant has been allowed to reach this condition, which we call "pot bound," it is best to lay the ball of roots on one hand and slap it smartly so as to loosen it; by this treatment the new fibres strike out more readily from the hard roots than if left with the ball still compact. After shifting a plant, give it one good watering, so that the soil will be thoroughly soaked to the bottom of the pot; but after that, keep rather dry until there are indications of new growth. For manner of potting, see chapter on "The Potting of Plants." We are often asked as to the use of guano and other fertilizers on in-door plants. As a general thing we use none in our own practice, preferring to shift the plants into fresh soil at the proper time, rather than to do so, and we would advise the same to our friends of less experience, for the use of all such stimulants is, under certain conditions of the plants, dangerous in unpracticed hands.

CHAPTER XX.

UNHEALTHY PLANTS—THE REMEDY.

Whenever plants begin to drop their leaves, it is certain that their health has been injured; this may be due to over-potting, over-watering, over-heating, too much cold,

or the application of such stimulants as guano, or to some
other cause which has destroyed the fine rootlets by which
the plant feeds, and induced disease that may lead to
death. The case is not usually important enough to call
in a " plant doctor," so the amateur begins to treat the
patient, and the practice is in all probability not unlike
that of many of our household physicians who apply a
remedy that increases the disease. Having already destroyed the, so to speak, nutritive organs of the plant,
the stomach is gorged with food by applying water, or
with medicine, by applying guano or some patent " plant
food." Now the remedy is nearly akin to what is a good
one when the animal digestion is deranged—give it no
more food until it re-acts. We must then, if the roots
of the plant have been injured from any of the above
named causes, let the soil in which it is potted become
nearly dry ; then remove the plant from the pot, take
the ball of soil in which the roots have been enveloped,
and crush it between the hands just enough to allow all
the sour outer crust of the ball of earth to be shaken off ;
then re-pot in rather dry soil, (composed of any fresh
soil mixed with equal bulk of leaf-mold or street sweepings), using a new flower-pot, or the old one, thoroughly washing it, so that the moisture can freely evap-
orate through the pores. Be careful not to over-feed the
sick plant. Let the pot be only large enough to admit
of not more than an inch of soil between the pot and ball
of roots. After re-potting, give it water enough to settle the soil, and do not apply any more until the plant
has begun to grow, unless indeed the atmosphere is so
dry that the moisture has entirely evaporated from the
soil, then of course water must be given, or the patient
may die from the opposite cause—starvation. The danger to be avoided is in all probability that which brought
on the sickness, namely : saturation of the soil by too
much water. Other causes may induce sickness in

plants, such as an escape of gas in the apartment, or smoke from a flue in the greenhouse, but in all cases, when the leaves fall from a plant, withhold water, and if there is reason to believe that the soil has been poisoned by gas, or soddened with moisture, shake it from the roots as before advised, and re-pot in a fresh flowerpot. Many years ago, when I used smoke-flues in my greenhouses, some kindling wood, carelessly thrown on the top of one of them, ignited, and the smoke caused the leaves of every plant to drop. There were some 3,000 plants, mostly Tea-Roses, in the greenhouse; it would have been too much of a job to re-pot all, but by withholding water for some ten days, they started a new growth again, and very few plants were injured.

CHAPTER XXI.

PLANTS SUITED FOR SUMMER DECORATION.

Quite a number of winter-blooming plants can also be used for flowering in the open borders in summer. Among these are Carnations, Heliotropes, Fuchsias, Geraniums, and particularly the monthly varieties of Roses. Also the following, not strictly winter-flowering, are such as will give a continuous bloom during the whole season, from June until October or November. Antirrhinums, (raised either from seeds or cuttings), Dwarf Dahlias, Erythrina or Coral Plant, Gladiolus, Geraniums of all kinds, particularly the class known as "Zonal," double and single, Lantanas, Lobelias, (seeds or cuttings), Petunias, single, (seeds or cuttings), Petunias, double; Pansies, (seeds only); Pentstemons, Passion-flowers, Rondeletias, Salvias, (seeds or cuttings); Tropæolums, (seeds or

cuttings); Verbenas, (seeds or cuttings); Veronicas. All of
the above have their principal attraction in their flowers.
The following are only useful for the brilliant coloring or other peculiarities of foliage.   Alternantheras,
Achyranthes, Artemisias, Cerastium, Centaureas, (seeds
or cuttings) ; Caladiums, Coleus, Cinerarias, (seeds or
cuttings); Dracænas, Echeverias, Geraniums,(silver, gold,
or bronze) ; variegated Ivies ; Lysimachia, variegated
Grasses ; Peristrophe, Sanchezia nobilis, Vinca major,
etc., etc.   For descriptions see florists' catalogues.   All
of the above can be raised from slips or cuttings taken
from plants, (or by seeds where noted), during the winter or early spring months—January, February, March,
or April, either from plants that have been kept for
flowering in winter, or from large plants that have been
preserved for the purpose of propagation ; the young
plants raised from slips are in nearly every instance
preferable to the old plants.   Our practice is, to grow
the old, or "stock" plants, simply to make cuttings, until
we get enough from them, and then to throw the old
plant away, reserving the young ones only for selling, or for our own planting in the open borders.
Cuttings are rooted in the way described in the chapter
on " Propagation of Plants by Cuttings," or if by seeds,
as in chapter on " Propagation by Seeds."   The young
plants should first be potted in 2-inch pots, and if early
in the season, they will require to be shifted into 3-inch
pots before it is time to plant them out in the open
ground, which it is not safe to do in this latitude until the
middle of May ; nor in any other latitude before the
time when tomatoes or egg plants can safely be planted out.
   Nothing is more satisfactory to the lover of flowers than
raising his own plants, no matter how able he may be to
purchase.   Those of his own raising, whether for his own
use or to present to his friends, are always more valuable than anything that money can buy.   One of the

most common mistakes made by purchasers of plants in our city markets, is that of almost invariably choosing large plants, *forced* into flower ; such plants are usually grown under a high temperature to get them in bloom early, and many a housewife has found that the beautiful full blooming plant of a Rose, Fuchsia, or Pelargonium, which she so tenderly carried home, will in 48 hours drop its flowers and leaves in the cooler and drier atmosphere of her greenhouse, parlor, or garden. But the florist is hardly to blame for this, though I know he is often severely censured ; not one in a score of those who purchase plants in spring will buy any plant unless it is in bloom ; the florist grows plants to sell, and must suit the wants of his customer. This partial divergence from the subject in hand, is to show that the small slips or cuttings that the amateur may raise himself, are in most instances better than full-blown forced plants, costing 50c. or $1 each. This is particularly so with monthly Roses, Verbenas, and Petunias ; young plants of these, set out in May, if not more than 3 or 6 inches high, will grow and bloom in profusion the entire summer, while those which have been forced, if they recover at all, will be greatly inferior.

We plant our young Roses in May, usually in beds 4 feet wide, setting the plants 12 inches apart each way ; they begin to bloom by the middle of June, and continue without interruption until checked by frost in the fall ; and so with most other kinds here named ; nearly all of which are from young plants, propagated during the winter and spring months. The product of cuttings or slips from a "stock" plant varies greatly according to the kind. A good healthy plant of Fuchsia, say 18 inches high, will easily give 40 cuttings ; while a Rose or Geranium of the same size will not afford half that number. A fair average for medium sized plants of those named would be 10 cuttings or slips to each plant, so that starting with 100 plants in the fall, by May 1,000 would be no unreasonable increase to expect ; or in that ratio be the number more or less.

If large quantities of plants are wanted for summer decoration by those who have neglected to propagate them, or did not wish to do so, they should purchase *young plants* in March or April, at which time the florists, to make room in their houses, sell them at very low rates, usually not more than one-fourth of the price that the same plants forced into bloom in May would cost. Such plants at that season are grown mainly in 2 and 3-inch pots ; if taken from these pots, say by 1st of April, and kept in any cool room or greenhouse, where the temperature will average 45° or 50° at night, by the time of setting out in May they will have formed far better plants than those pushed rapidly into flower in May. Or in other words, $10 expended in March or April, will buy one hundred plants, which, if cared for as above described, will by the middle of May be of more value than the plants $50 would buy at that date from the same florist.

CHAPTER XXII.

HANGING BASKETS.

Baskets in which to grow plants are now made in a great variety of styles, and of different materials. What are known as " rustic " baskets, (fig. 26), are made with the receptacle for the earth covered mostly with laurel roots, which assume an endless variety of grotesque shapes, well fitted for giving a rustic appearance to the outer covering of the hanging basket. Then there are the different forms of wire baskets, (fig. 27), which, when used, are lined with moss, and being thus very open, and allowing of complete drainage, are best suited of all for the well being of the plants. A recent invention is the "Balloon" hanging basket, (fig. 28), the trellis part of which is formed of strips of steel; some are so arranged as to hold a common flower-pot. Many

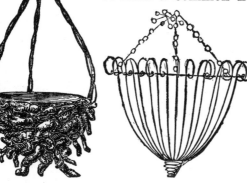

beautiful forms are made from pottery ware, colored so as to imitate stumps of wood and other objects. Thousands of these baskets are used in some of their different forms, and

Fig. 26.
RUSTIC HANGING BASKET.

Fig. 27.
WIRE BASKET.

many grow their plants in no other way, as plants are not only more easily managed in these, but many varieties so cultivated make a more graceful growth than is possible when they are in pots. In hanging baskets, the fall, or Dutch bulbs, of all kinds, can be grown, giving them exactly the treatment recommended for growing in pots on page 36. When hanging baskets are hung on the veranda or porch in summer, a great quantity of water is usually required, as the dry air surrounding the basket on all sides generally drys up the soil. The simplest way of watering

Fig. 28.—BALLOON FRAME.

them when dry, in summer, is to immerse the basket in a

4

pail or tub of water, so that the earth is thoroughly soaked
through ; how often this immerson will be necessary will
depend on the weather, the condition of the plants
and the quantity of earth.   If the bowl of the basket is
full of roots, and the weather hot and dry, then once
each day may be necessary ; while if the weather is damp
and cool, it might not require watering more than once
a week.   The rule with these as with all plants is—never
water unless they are dry, and then water *thoroughly.*
Just what this condition of being " dry " is, is not quite
so easy to describe ; as a rule most soils when dry become
lighter in color and crumble freely between the fingers,
and are free from the putty-like consistency they have
when wet.   The bowls of " rustic " and " Terra Cotta "
forms of hanging baskets are usually without any holes
for drainage ;   when such is the case, the purchaser
should have a few holes, say one-fourth inch in diameter,
made in the bottom of the bowl, else there is danger that the earth around the roots may become saturated with water, unless unusual care is taken in watering.
There is great diversity of taste displayed in the material
with which these baskets are filled, and no special list of
plants can be given that will not require to be annually
changed and amended as new plants are introduced.
When hanging baskets are wanted for use in shady rooms,
or on shaded verandas, mosses, (selaginellas), are used,
and sometimes exclusively.   Then for the same conditions, Ivies of all sorts, Cissus, Tradescantias, Sedums or
Stone Crops, Fittonias, Lysimachia or Moneywort, Vincas, Ivy-leaved Geraniums, Smilax, etc., as plants to
droop over the sides, or to be trained to climb on the
trellis work or supports of the basket, while in the center
there are used upright plants, such as Dracænas of sorts,
Caladiums, (if for summer), Marantas, Centaureas,
Echeverias, Ferns, Sanchezia nobilis, and other plants of
striking form or foliage.   For baskets to be placed in the

sun, or in good light, an entirely different class of plants is needed, for with the light we get flowers. As drooping plants for the edges of these, may be named Alternantheras, Peristrophe angustifolia var., Lobelias, Tropæolums, Mesembryanthemums, Petunias, single and double ; Passifloras, Rondeletias, Torrenias, etc., while for upright or center plants, Achyranthes, Coleus, Begonias, Geraniums, Zonal, double, single, and variegated leaved, or any plant of not too large a growth, and which has brightness of foliage or flower. If hanging baskets are exposed to the full rays of the sun, or even partially so, covering the surface of the soil with moss from the woods will protect it from drying too quickly, and will also give the basket a neater appearance. The soil used for hanging baskets need in no way differ from that for plants grown in pots.

CHAPTER XXIII.

WINDOW GARDENING.

Window gardening during the summer months is much more successful in England than with us, owing to a more temperate climate, and hence is there almost universally practised. In the cities especially, where space is economized by placing story upon story, and the buildings are so close that there is often no room for even a spear of grass to be grown, the only garden that is possible is one formed in a box on the window-sill; this is limited in its extent, as the space afforded is only some 4 or 5 feet in length, from 8 to 10 inches wide, with a depth for the soil of about 6 inches. These boxes, are made of a great variety of materials, such as wood, terra cotta, iron, etc., according to the taste or means of the owner. As the boxes are usually too high up to allow of a close examination, and the sides soon become draped with dropping plants, an ordinary box of pine, as in fig. 29, will answer as well as a more expensive one; as it is exposed to the weather, and the weight of the earth is considerable, it should be put to-

Fig. 29.—PLAIN WINDOW-BOX.

gether very firmly. Having procured the box, then let a tinsmith make a lining or box of zinc that will exactly fit inside of it ; this needs only a few tacks at the upper edge to hold the zinc to the wood. A more expensive box, (fig. 30), is made of wood, lined with zinc, and the exterior covered with ornamental tiles, which are kept in place by a proper molding at the margins. A box of this kind may be covered with floor oil-cloth, and if a proper pattern be selected, it cannot at a few yards off be told from the much more costly tiles. Many of the streets

Fig. 30.—WINDOW-BOX ORNAMENTED WITH TILES.

of London and Edinburgh, during the summer months, present a pleasing appearance, that cannot fail to inter-est even those who have no taste for flowers. The plants used are mainly such as we recommend for hanging bas-kets, those designated for shady positions being used on the shady sides of the streets, and those for flowering on the sunny sides. These window gardens in summer produce

the finest effect when planted with some drooping species. For our climate, during the summer months,
when exposed to full sun, strong, vigorous-growing
plants must be selected, such as Tropæolums, Petunias,
Passifloras, etc. While for the same position, the upright
plants may be double and single Geraniums, Heliotropes,
Mignonnette, and the like. For window boxes on the shady
side, use the plants recommended for hanging baskets in
shade. The soil may be such as is used for pots. Watering must be given as recommended for hanging baskets, only in the case of the window box it would not be
practicable to immerse it, nor is there the same necessity
for doing so, as the box is less exposed than the hanging
basket, which is suspended and surrounded by drying
air upon all sides. These remarks refer to window gardening outside of the windows, or on the outer sill. If
the boxes are placed inside in winter, which they may
be, the treatment recommended in chapter on "Winter
Flowering Plants," will be applicable.

CHAPTER XXIV.

PARLOR GARDENING, OR THE CULTIVATION OF PLANTS IN ROOMS.

Parlor Gardening has to some extent been treated of
under the head of winter flowering plants, but a few additional general directions for plants not specially designed for winter flowering, may be acceptable. One of
the first conditions essential to success is to start with
healthy plants. Even all the professional skill of the
florist, with all his appliances, will often fail to get a
sickly plant into a healthy condition. What then can

the amateur florist expect to do in the often unequal temperature and dry atmosphere of a sitting room or parlor ? If the plants are purchased from the florist in autumn, to grow in the house, they are likely to be healthy, and are usually in a condition to shift into a pot one size larger ; instructions for doing this are given in the chapter on "Winter Flowering Plants." But if the plants to be cultivated in the house are such as have been growing in your own flower borders, plants that were set out in spring, and have now the full summer's luxuriant growth still on them, then proper precaution must be taken in lifting them and placing them in pots, or the result is certain to be most unsatisfactory. What may seem to the novice a little singular, is, that the more luxuriant the growth of the plant in the open border, the more danger there is that it will wilt or die when lifted in the fall, and placed in a pot. The reason of this is obvious, when it is known that just in proportion to the top growth of a plant is the wide-spread development of roots, and therefore when you lift a finely-grown Geranium or Rose in October, it is next to impossible, if it is to be got into a suitable sized flower-pot, to do so without such mutilation of the young roots as will certainly kill it, if precaution is not taken to cut off at least two-thirds of its branches. If the plant is thus potted and kept as dry as it will stand without actually withering, until it starts growth, you may hope to have a fairly healthy specimen by December, if the lifting was done in October. But this practice, though often one of necessity, is never satisfactory. If the plants that have done service in the borders in summer are to be used as ornaments for the parlor in fall, winter, and spring, they must have a different treatment. All plants that are intended for future culture in rooms, should be potted in the usual way, into 5 or 6-inch pots, when set out in May or June ; these pots should be set in the flower borders, but planted or "plunged," as it is called, so that the rim of the pot is level with the surface of the ground. The plants will flower if so desired, in these pots, nearly as well as if set directly in the open ground, but if wanted for flowering in winter, they will bloom much better to have the flower-buds picked off as fall approaches. It is also indispensably necessary that the hole in the bottom of the pot be entirely stopped, so that the roots cannot get through. The object being to confine the roots completely within the bounds of the pot, so that when taken up in the fall to be shifted into a larger pot, the roots will be undisturbed, and the plant will grow on unchecked. If this is not done, and the roots find their way through the bottom of the pot, there will be the same difficulty with the roots as if they had not been potted. About the best time to take plants in-doors in this climate is the middle of October; in colder localities, earlier, of course, and in warmer, later; always bearing in mind that the longer they can be kept in the open air, provided they are safe from frost, the better. Plants suited for parlor culture, requiring a temperature of from 40° to 50° at night, with an average of 10° or 20° higher during the day are as follows. These are known as greenhouse plants. For descriptions see catalogues of florists and nurserymen.

Acacias,	Cupheas,
Azaleas,	Daphnes,
*Agapathus,	*Echeverias,
*Alternantheras,	Ferns, Greenhouse,
*Agaves,	Feverfews,
*Abutilons,	*Fuchsias,
*Achyranthes,	Geraniums—Pelargoniums,
Ageratums,	Hoyas, (wax plant),
*Callas,	Holland Bulbs of all kinds,
Calceolarias,	*Jessamines —Catalonian,
Chorizema,	Jessamines—Cape,
Cinerarias,	Ivies—parlor and hardy,
*Carnations,	*Ixoras,
Cyclamen,	Lily of the Valley,
Camellias,	Lobelias,

*Mesembryanthemums, (wax pink),   *Primulas, double and single,
Mahernias,   *Roses,
Mimulus—Musk,   *Scutellarias,
*Myrsiphyllum, or Smilax,   Veronicas,
Oranges,   Vincas,
Oleanders,   Violets,
Petunias,   Yuccas.
Pinks,

What are known as hot-house, or tropical plants, require a higher temperature than the preceeding, and cannot be well grown unless with a night temperature of from 60° to 70°, and a day temperature of from 10° to 20° higher. The following, of most of which there are several varieties, can be found described in the catalogues of dealers :

Allamandas,   Ferns, tropical,
Allocasias,   Heliotropes,
Begonias,   Hibiscus,
Bouvardias,   Marantas,
Caladiums,   Orchids, (of some kinds),
Cissus,   Passifloras,
Clerodendrons,   Peperomias,
Cobæas,   Poinsettia,
Crotons,   Salvias,
Coleus,   Sanchezias,
Dracænas,   Torenias,
Euphorbias,   Tropæolums,
Epiphyllums—Cactus,   Tuberoses.
Eranthemums,

This matter of temperature has everything to do with the successful cultivation of plants in rooms, or in fact anywhere. If you attempt, for example, to grow Bouvardias or Begonias in an average temperature of 45° at night, the plants will barely live, and will not flower, nor be healthy. On the other hand, if you subject your Camellias or Geraniums to an average of 65° at night by fire heat in winter, you are almost certain to have the flowers drop prematurely. As a rule, there are more of the plants known as greenhouse that will endure the high temperature necessary for the hot-house plants, than there are of the hot-house plants that can stand the low temperature, so when no distinction can be made, and a high temperature only can be had, all in the list of greenhouse plants I have marked with a * may be grown fairly in the high temperature, though they would do better in the low one. The culture of plants in rooms is already described in the chapter on " Winter Flowering Plants," so that I need not further allude to it, except to hint in regard to the manner of placing the plants. One of the cheapest and neatest contrivances is the "folding plant stand," (fig. 31). The sizes are from 3 to 6 feet wide, and 8 feet high, having from 4 to 6 shelves, and capable of holding from 25 to 100 plants. It is hinged so as to fold up like a camp stool,

Fig. 31.—FOLDING PLANT STAND.

the shelves fitting in between the frames, and can be thus shipped or stowed away when not wanted, with great convenience. Rollers can be attached to the feet, so that it may be moved about as easily as a table. Plants, when placed on this, or similar stands, may be provided with saucers, so that the floor or carpet need not be injured while watering. It is not a good plan, however, to keep water in the saucers. It is always a safer way of feeding the plant to water the soil on the top, giving only enough for it to reach the bottom, where, if any water pass through, it will be held by the saucer. If no saucers are used, and we think plants are generally grown more safely without them, the best plan is, to take down the plants from the stand, (three times a week will usually be enough), to some place where the water will not do any injury, and give all such as appear to be dry, a good soaking ; those not so dry, water more sparingly, and give those in which the soil shows that it is wet, none whatever. Let the water drain off, pick off any dead leaves, and replace the pots again on the stand, being careful to change them as far as possible, so that each side of the plant may get its fair share of light ; if the same part is always placed to the light, the plant will soon become drawn to one side.

CHAPTER XXV.

WARDIAN CASES, FERNERIES, AND JARDINIERES.

The forms of plant cases for the growth of such plants as require a moist, still atmosphere, a condition impossible to obtain in a room in a dwelling-house, nor even in a greenhouse, unless it is specially erected for the purpose, are numerous. The form commonly known as the Wardian Case, (fig. 32), has a base or tray usually of black walnut, about 6 inches deep, and lined with zinc, and glass sides and top ; these differ in size, some being as large as 3 feet on the sides. Another neat and cheaper form is made of Terra Cotta, (fig. 33), or other earthen ware ; these are usually round in shape, and of various

Fig. 32.—WARDIAN CASE.

sizes, from 9 to 18 inches in diameter. In all these the plants must be covered with glass ; in the Wardian Case there is glass all around the sides and top, the top being hinged to allow the escape of excess of moisture. In the Jardinieres, or circular form, the plants are covered by a bell-glass which is tilted up a little at the side, when there is an appearance of excess of moisture. This condition of excess is known by the glass becoming dimmed by moisture, and the water trickling down the side. Usually when this appearance is seen, by raising the glass lid of the Wardian Case an inch or so for a day, it will relieve it enough to enable it to be kept close, which is the proper way to keep it for the well being of the plants. The plants grown in this way are of kinds valued for their beauty of foliage, rather than for their flowers, and should be such as are rather of a slow growth; all rampant growing plants, such as Coleus, are unsuited. The

Fig. 33.—FERNERY WITH GLASS SHADE.

effectiveness of these cases depend a great deal on the arrangement of the plants; the tallest and most conspicuous things should be in the center, with smaller ones towards the edges, varying the interest by contrasting the different colorings and forms of leaves. Among the plants best suited for growing under these glass coverings, are Dracænas, Gymnostachyums, Marantas, Caladiums, some of the ornamental leaved Eranthemums, and dwarf growing Begonias, Peperomias, etc., and Ferns and Lycopods of the finer sorts. The most of these are plants whose natural habitat is shady woods or marshes; and for their well being, the nearest that the Wardian Case or Jardiniere can be made to imitate such, the better.

The soil used in these cases should be light and porous. The most convenient, and a very suitable material, is the leaf-mold, which can be got in any piece of woodland. After planting, the soil should be watered freely, so that it is settled around the roots. And to allow evaporation, ventilation should be given for a few days after the watering, when the glass may be put down close, only to be opened as before directed, when an excess of moisture shows on the glass. Other than this there is no trouble whatever in the management; the watering given on planting will be sufficient to keep it moist enough for 6 or 8 weeks. In winter the temperature of the room in which the Wardian case or fernery is kept may run from 50° to 70° at night. These closed cases of either kind may be used for growing Hyacinths in winter if desired, for which they are particularly well adapted; only, that when brought into the room to flower, the cases will require daily ventilation. After planting the Hyacinths in the cases, however, it must not be forgotten that they must be kept in a cool, dark place, until they root, just as when they are grown in pots, or glasses. For further instructions on this head see Hyacinths. Lily of the Valley can also be grown finely in a Wardian case; but as it requires some special treatment, we give it in a separate chapter.

CHAPTER XXVI.

WINTER FORCING THE LILY OF THE VALLEY.

Within the past three years the fashion for the flowers of Lily of the Valley has increased to such an extent, that though the importation of roots has probably trebled each year, the price of the flower is still quite as high as when the forcing first begun. The failures which attend the winter flowering of this plant are mainly owing to the use of improperly developed roots. As with other similar plants, a certain size or development of the crown, or underground bud, is essential to produce the flower. What that size should be, is not, even with the most experienced, always easy to determine. In the Tuberose, the Japan, and some other Lilies, we find that bulbs that are less than an inch in diameter, are not certain to

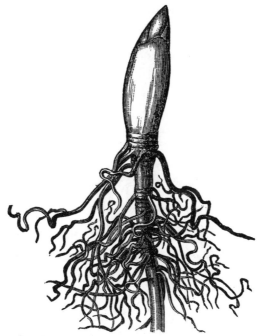

Fig. 34.—LILY OF THE VALLEY BUD—GOOD.

flower. The crown, or "pip," as florists sometimes call it, of the Lily of the Valley, when sufficiently developed to flower, should be of the size and shape shown in fig. 34. Those too small to flower are like that shown in fig. 35. But these rules as to size and shape are not given as certain, for few have had experience enough to say with accuracy at what size the crown of the Lily of the Valley will *not* flower, although we may say with some certainty, if the crown is large, that it will do so. It is the want of this knowledge that, in my opinion, has made the flowering of the Lily of the Valley so uncertain when forced. As in forcing the Hyacinth, and other similar bulbs, crowns of the Lily of the Valley should be covered up outside for a few weeks, before being brought into the greenhouse or house to force. Those we flower are put in about the middle of November, packed closely together in light, rich soil, in boxes three inches deep. These are covered up outside with hay until the first of

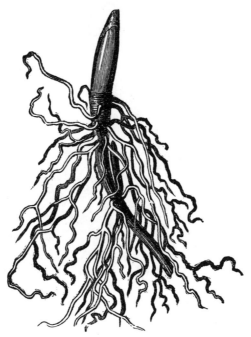

Fig. 35.—LILY OF THE VALLEY BUD—POOR.

January; they are then brought into a greenhouse, facing north, where there is no direct sunlight at that season. The temperature is kept at about 70°, with a moist atmosphere, and by the first of February they are in full flower. The Lily of the Valley could be grown finely in a Wardian case, as it would there get the proper light, with the necessary damp atmosphere. When grown in greenhouses, exposed to sunlight, it is necessary to shade the glass very heavily. When the flowers are about to open, they should then have light to give the leaves a healthy green color.

CHAPTER XXVII.

GREENHOUSES ATTACHED TO DWELLINGS.

The taste engendered by growing plants in rooms often results in a desire to have more appropriate quarters for the plants, and a greenhouse follows. This always affords the most satisfaction when it is so attached to the dwelling that opening a door or window from the dining-room or parlor, reveals the glories of the greenhouse. The greenhouse, when attached to the dwelling, should be always on the east, south-east, south, or south-west sides, never on the north. It may be of any length or width desired. If of ten feet width, it will cost for erection from $4 to $6 per running foot, according to the character of the work. If 20 feet wide, from $8 to $10 per running foot. This is exclusive of heating, which, if done by hot-water pipes, will cost for 10 feet wide, about $4 per running foot; if 20 feet wide, about $8 per running foot. Thus to complete a conservatory, with heating apparatus, shelves, etc., 10 feet wide by 40 feet long, it would cost about $400; if 20 x 40 feet, about $800. In this estimate it is assumed that the heating is to be done by the Base Burning Water-heater, of Hitchings & Co. This heating apparatus is of recent invention, and is exceedingly well adapted for the purpose, as the fire requires no more attention than any ordinary base burning stoves. The boiler takes up no more room than an ordinary stove, and requires no set-

ting; it is shown in fig. 36, and in section in fig. 37. It is
fed by coal from the top, and can be left with safety 10
or 12 hours without any attention. It must be borne in
mind that in constructing the conservatory it must be
built where a chimney is accessible by which to carry off
the smoke from the boiler or water heater, just as would

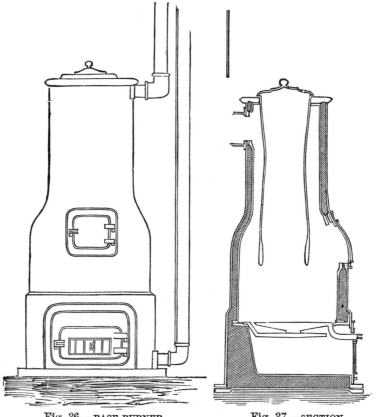

Fig. 36.—BASE-BURNER.   Fig. 37.—SECTION.

be necessary for an ordinary stove. If the greenhouse is small enough to be heated from a register from
the furnace that heats the dwelling, much of the cost
may be saved, as it will be seen that nearly half of the
cost of construction is the heating apparatus. Figure
38 shows a front elevation of a conservatory suitable to

Fig. 38.—ELEVATION OF CONSERVATORY ATTACHED TO DWELLING.

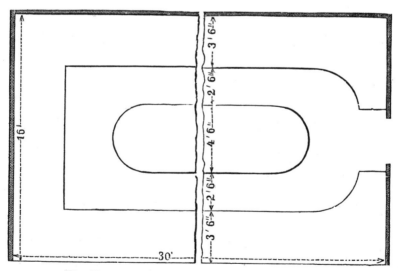

Fig. 39.—GROUND PLAN OF CONSERVATORY, FIG. 38.

attach to dwellings ; this is 16 feet wide and 30 feet in length. Its ground plan showing the arrangement of the benches and walks, is given in fig. 39. Such a structure in every way complete, heated with Hitchings Base Burning water-heater, should not exceed $600.

———◦◦◦———

CHAPTER XXVIII.

A DETACHED GREENHOUSE OR GRAPERY.

In cases where more extended glass structures are desired, they are better if detached from the dwelling. The structure now given in figs. 40 and 41 is called a curvilinear span-roofed house, 100 feet in length by 20 in width ; fig. 40 shows the end view and plan, and fig. 41 gives sufficient of the elevation to show the end and a part of the side. The ends should face north and south, so that the distribution of the sun's rays will be equal on each side. Of course there is nothing arbitrary in the size, it may be made 50, 75, or 100 feet in length, or 20 to 25 feet in width as desired, and may be used either for the purposes of a vinery for the growing of foreign grapes, or for a conservatory as desired. All the walling from the surface of the ground to the glass of a greenhouse, had better be made of wood, unless the walls are made very thick when built of brick or stone ; the continued warfare in winter between a zero temperature outside, and 60° to 70° inside, will in a year or two destroy brick or stone walls. When the walls are formed of wood, the best way is to place locust posts at distances of four feet apart, and nail to these a sheathing of boards ; against the boards tack asphaltum or tarred paper, and again against that, place the weather-boarding. This forms a wall

SCALE

Fig. 40.—END-VIEW AND PLAN OF DETACHED GREENHOUSE OR GRAPERY.

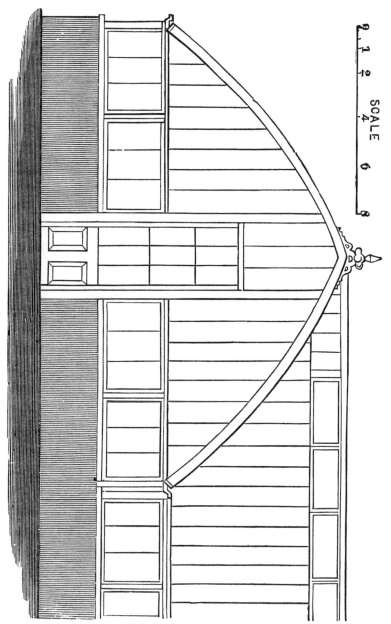

Fig. 41.—ELEVATION (IN PART) OF DETACHED GREENHOUSE OR GRAPERY.

which, if kept painted, will last for 50 years, and is equally warm as a 12-inch brick wall, and costs less than half. We have had just such a structure in use for the past five years as a cold vinery, that is having no heating apparatus, the forwarding being done only by the action of the sun on the glass, and it has proved a cheap and satisfactory luxury. A conservatory or grapery of this style costs from $10 to $15 per running foot, without heating apparatus. Heated by hot water, it would cost $20 to $30 per running foot. If heated by a horizontal flue in the manner here described, the cost will be only about $15 per running foot. Any good bricklayer should be able to build a smoke-flue from the following instructions. Let the bars for the grate be, (if for a glass surface of say 500 square feet), 2 feet in length and about 10 inches in width ; or in the proportion of about one-half a square inch of grate surface to one square foot of glass.

Most masons of any experience know how to build a greenhouse flue, but there are a few important points, the knowledge of which is absolutely necessary to complete success. First, the furnace pit, if not naturally dry, must be made so by draining. After setting the grate-bars in the usual way by resting them on an iron plate, let into the brick work at front and back, the sides of the furnace should be built with fire-brick and fire clay if at all procurable, to the hight of from 10 to 20 inches, according to size wanted. On these walls an arch is turned over to cover the furnace ; the " neck " of the furnace rising at a sharp angle for from 2 to 4 feet until it is run into the horizontal smoke-flue. The flue must be raised from the ground an inch or two on bricks or flagging. This costs perhaps a third more in building, but it allows all sides of the flue to give off heat. The cheapest and simplest form of flue is made after the bottom is formed by bricks or flagging ; brick is best near the furnace, as flagging would crack. Place two bricks on edge, the top being covered by a brick laid flat; this is the smallest size of flue. Larger grate surface will require correspondingly greater hight and breadth. Flues are now commonly made by using cement or vitrified drain pipe, to connect with the brick flue, at from 25 to 40 feet from the furnace, the pipe not being safe to use near the furnace, as the greater heat would be likely to crack it. A flue, to get the full benefit of the fuel, should be so arranged that it goes all around the greenhouse, the base of the chimney being the top of the furnace. The advantage of this plan, (fig. 42), which has only recently had general publicity, is that the excessive heat given out from the top of the furnace, drives back the cold air that would otherwise pass down the chimney; not only

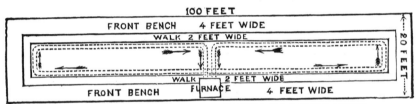

Fig. 42.—PLAN OF GREENHOUSE HEATED BY DOUBLE FLUES.

drives it back, but passing rapidly out, "draws" to it the heated air that has to pass through the length of the horizontal flue, causing it to circulate so rapidly that all parts of the flue become nearly equally heated. In the case represented in fig. 42, the greenhouse so heated is 20 feet wide by 100 feet long, having a glass surface of over 2,500 square feet, a size utterly impossible to heat with a flue unless so constructed that the base of the chimney stands on the top of the furnace. It will be seen by the plan that there are two flues running from one furnace, and entering into one chimney. I only illustrate this to show the power given by this method. It would do quite as well, if the house was half or quarter the size, to have it done by one flue instead of the two. I would here say emphatically that no matter what size a flue may be, and whether single or double, it should in every case be made on the principle of being carried all around the building until it enters the upright chimney built on the top of the furnace.

———◦◇◦———

CHAPTER XXIX.

HEATING BY HOT WATER.

Although we describe flues as a means of heating greenhouses or graperies, they should be used only on the score of economy; whenever one can afford to have the heating done in the best manner, by all means let it be done by hot water. The hot-water apparatus requires less attention than flues, and its management is so simple that any one able to take care of an ordinary stove or furnace can take charge of a boiler for heating the water in the pipes of a greenhouse. Besides, there is no danger from smoke or gas, and but little risk from fire. Inside the greenhouse there is no danger from fire; if they are filled with water the pipes cannot be made hot enough to ignite the most combustible substances that may come in contact with them. With the smoke flue it is very different, dry wood or other combustible material will ignite if allowed to touch the brick, anywhere within 20 to 40 feet of the furnace. There are a great many patterns of boilers, and to recommend one more than another may seem invidious; still we have had in use quite a number of different styles, and have found that, as far as our experience with them has gone, those made by Hitchings & Co., of New York, everything considered, have been most satisfactory. We have several of these boilers in use that have not cost a dollar for repair in ten years.

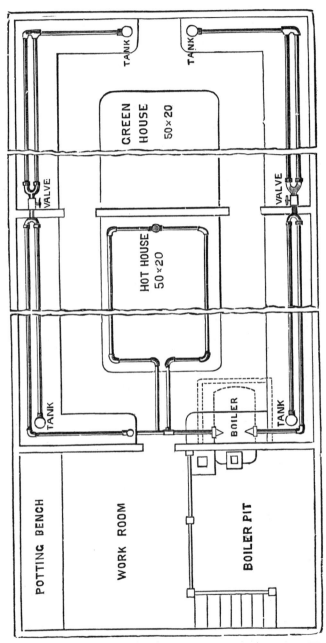

Fig. 43.— PLAN OF HOT-HOUSE AND GREENHOUSE COMBINED.

Figure 43 gives the ground plan of a combined hot-house and greenhouse, each 20 feet wide and 50 feet long, showing the disposition of the boiler and pipes. If this plan were shown in full on the page, the width would be quite too small, therefore a portion of the length is left out of each compartment, as shown by the irregular lines; everything is given in proper proportion except the length, and that is stated in figures. The number of pipes indicated, (10), is sufficient to give a temperature of from 60° to 70° at night for the hot-

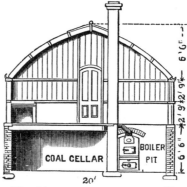

Fig. 44.—END-VIEW OF FIG. 43, AT BOILER PIT.

house, and the number given in the greenhouse, (6), is such as will keep that compartment at from 40° to 50° in the coldest weather. A sectional view at the end where

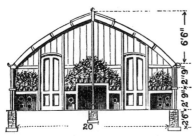

Fig. 45.—END-VIEW OF FIG. 43, AT PARTITION BETWEEN THE TWO HOUSES.

the boiler pit is placed is given in fig. 44, and another sectional view at the partition between the greenhouse and hot-house is shown in fig. 45. The cost of such a structure complete for the reception of plants, would vary according to location, and the style of finish; in the vicinity of New York at present prices, such a combined hot-house and greenhouse, 20x100, erected in a substantial manner, would cost about $3,000.

CHAPTER XXX.

GREENHOUSES OR PITS, WITHOUT ARTIFICIAL HEATING.

The directions given for heating greenhouses by hot water or by flues, apply of course only to sections of the country where the temperature during the winter months makes heating a necessity. In many of the southern states there is no need of artificial heat. A greenhouse tightly glazed and placed against a building where it is sheltered from the north and north-west will keep out frost when the temperature does not fall lower than 25 degrees *above* zero, and if light wooden shutters are used to cover the glass, all those classed as "greenhouse" plants will be safe even at 10 degrees lower, provided, of course, that the conservatory is attached to the dwelling, as shown in fig. 38. Another cheap and simple method of keeping plants during winter in mild latitudes is by

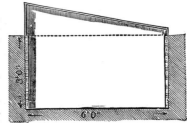

Fig. 46.—SUNKEN PIT.

the use of the sunken pit or deep frame, which affords the needed protection even more completely than the elevated greenhouse. This is formed by excavating the soil to the depth of from 18 to 36 inches, according to the size of the plants it is intended to contain. A convenient width is 6 feet, the ordinary length of a hot-bed sash, and of such length as may be desired. Great care must be taken that the ground is such that no water will stand in the pit ; if the soil is moist it should be drained. The sides of the pit may be either walled up by a 4 or 8-inch course of brick work, or planked up as may be preferred, but in either case the *back* wall should be raised about eighteen inches, and the front about six inches above the surface, in order to give the necessary slope to receive the sun's rays and to shed the water. A section of such a pit is shown in fig. 46. If a pit of this kind is made in a dry and sheltered position, and the glass covered by light shutters of half-inch boards, it may be used to keep all the hardier class of greenhouse plants, even in localities where the thermometer falls to zero.

CHAPTER XXXI.

COMBINED CELLAR AND GREENHOUSE.

In connection with the description of the cold pit or greenhouse without fire heat, may be mentioned the combined cellar and greenhouse. Many years ago an accidental circumstance gave me an opportunity of testing the utility of such a structure. An excavation of 20 feet by 40 had been made 7 feet deep, and walled up with stone and beams laid across preparatory to placing a building upon it, when the owner changed his plans and found himself with this useless excavation within a dozen yards of his costly residence. There seemed to be no alternative but to fill it up or plank it over, but both plans were objectionable, and in discussing how to get out of the difficulty, I suggested erecting a low-roofed greenhouse over it, as the owner had a taste for cultivating plants. This suggestion was followed, and the walls were raised one foot above the surface and a span-roofed greenhouse erected over it.

My idea, (which was found to be nearly correct), was, that the large volume of air in the excavation would at no season go below 40°, and be sufficient to keep the upper or greenhouse portion of the structure above the freezing point in the coldest weather. This it did completely when the glass was covered at night with shutters ; and the plants with which it was filled, of a kind requiring a low temperature, kept in better health than if they had been grown in a greenhouse having fire heat.

Now, although I have never seen such a combination since, I am satisfied that in favorable circumstances such a structure might be made of great utility and at a trifling cost, for as it dispenses with heating apparatus, which usually is more than half of the whole cost in all greenhouses, the use of a cellar and greenhouse could be had at probably less than the cost of an ordinary greenhouse ; and for half hardy plants—plants that will do well in winter if kept only above the freezing point—such a greenhouse will be better for many of them than any kind of greenhouse heated by fire heat. All kinds of Roses, Camellias, Azaleas, Zonal Geraniums, Violets, Cape Jessamines, Carnations, Abutilons, Verbenas, Primulas, Stevias, and, in short, all plants known as cool greenhouse plants, will keep in a healthy, though nearly dormant condition, during the winter months, but they will flourish with greatly increased vigor at their natural season of growth, and flowering as spring advances. Besides, the cellar may be used for the ordinary purposes of such a place ; or if exclusively for horticultural purposes, no better place can be had for keeping all deciduous hardy or half hardy plants, Hyacinths in pots to start to flower, or any bulbs of similar nature. The great point to be observed is that the soil where such a structure is to be erected is entirely free from water, or if not so naturally, must be made entirely dry by draining.

The style that I think would suit best for general purposes would be twelve feet in width, and of any length desired. The excavation should not be less than seven feet deep, walled up to about one foot above the surface. When complete it would show something like the section in fig. 47. If the glass roof is made fixed it should have ventilating sashes 3 x 3, at intervals of six or nine feet on each side of the roof ; if of sashes, they should be seven feet long by three feet wide, every alternate one being arranged to move for ventilation in the usual way. The position of the structure would be best with its ends north

Fig. 47.—GREENHOUSE AND CELLAR COMBINED.

and south. The shutters for covering the glass at night should be made of light half-inch pine boards, three feet wide by seven feet long.

It will be understood that the advantage of this combination of cellar and greenhouse over the ordinary cold pit is that the air of the greenhouse is warmed or equalized by mixing with the atmosphere of the cellar, which will rarely be less than 40°. For the same reason, if a high temperature by fire heat were wanted, say 70°, this large body of air from below of 40° would make it difficult to obtain it. It will be necessary, of course, to have the flooring boards covering the cellar wide enough apart to freely allow the passage of the air; this will at the same time give light enough for any operations necessary to be done in the cellar.

CHAPTER XXXII.

HOT-BEDS.

The sunken pit described on page 98 may be readily converted into a hot-bed; all that is necessary to do being to place hot manure or other heating material in the pit and tread it moderately firm with the feet. The manure should fill the pit to the depth of two feet, and then be covered with five or six inches of light rich soil, on which to sow the seed. This sunken pit prevents the escape of heat from the manure much better than when the hot-bed is made on the surface in the usual way. The preparation of the heating material for the hot-bed requires some attention. It should be manure fresh from the horse-stable, and when they can be procured, it is better to mix it with about an equal bulk of leaves from the woods. If the weather is very cold, the bulk of manure must be of good size, from five to six wagon loads, thrown in a compact conical heap, else the mass may be so chilled that fermentation cannot take place and no heat generated. If a shed is convenient, the manure may be placed there, especially if the quantity is small, to be protected from cold until the heat begins to rise. The heap should be turned and well broken up before being used for the hot-beds, so that the rank steam may escape and the manure become of the proper "sweetened" condition for the healthy germination of the seeds. After the manure has been packed in the pit to the depth and in the manner described, the sashes should be placed on the frame and kept close until the heat is again generated in the hot-bed. Now plunge a thermometer into the manure, and if all is right it will indicate 100 degrees or more, but this is yet too hot as bottom heat for the growth of seeds or plants, and a few days of delay must be allowed until the thermometer indicates a falling of 10 or 15 degrees, then the soil may be placed upon the manure and the seeds sown, or plants set out in the hot-bed. Amateurs are apt to be impatient in the matter of hot-beds, and often lose their first crop by sowing or planting before the first violent heat has subsided. Another very common mistake is, in beginning too early in the season. In this latitude nothing is gained by beginning before the first week in March, and the result will be very nearly as good if not begun until a month later. There are two or three important matters to bear in mind in the use of hot-beds. It is indispensable for safety to cover the glass at night with shutters or mats until all danger of frost is over, for it must be remembered that the contents of a hot-bed are always tender from being forced so rapidly by the heat below, and that the slightest frost will kill them. Again, there is danger of overheating in day-time by a neglect to ventilate when the sun is shining. As a general rule it will be safe in all the average days of March, April, and May, to have the sash in the hot-bed tilted up from an inch to three inches at the back from 9 A.M. to 4 P.M. Much will, of course, depend upon the activity of the heating material in the hot-bed, the warmth of the weather, and the character of the plants in the bed ; so that we can only give a loose general rule. Numbers of our amateur friends come to us every season lamenting that themselves or their men in charge had omitted to ventilate their hot-bed, and on their return home from business at night, found all the contents had been " boiled " up. Or the complaint may be on the other extreme, that the plants are frozen through neglect to cover them at night. A hot-bed requires a certain amount of attention, which must be given at the right time, or failure is certain.

CHAPTER XXXIII.

SHRUBS, CLIMBERS, AND TREES.

A place is seldom so small that a few choice shrubs
cannot appropriately find room, and in which climbers
are not desirable, while in the larger places these become
important to its proper ornamentation. Whether its size
admits of the use of trees or not, both deciduous and
evergreen shrubs, climbers as well as evergreen trees of
low growth, are indispensable. We here append a list of
the leading kinds in each class, but which by no means
exhausts the number of desirable varieties ; for the others reference may be made to the catalogues of the principal nurseries, where also will be found descriptions of
those here named.

HARDY DECIDUOUS SHRUBS.

Amygdalus nana fl. pl. ....Flowering Almond.
Æsculus parviflora ....Dwarf Horsechestnut.
Berberis vulgaris ....Barberry.
    "   "   *var. purpurea*.. ....Purple Barberry.
Calycanthus floridus ....Sweet-scented Shrub.
Chionanthus Virginica ....Fringe Tree.
Cytisus elongatus ....Laburnum.
Cotoneaster microphylla ....Small-leaved Cotoneaster.
Cratægus Pyracantha ....Pyracanth Thorn.
    "   *oxyacantha fl. pl.* ....Hawthorn double white.
    "   " *coccinea fl. pl* ..... "   " Scarlet.
Clethra alnifolia. ....White Alder.
Deutzia scabra ....Rough Deutzia.
    "   *crenata fl. pl* ....Double   "
    "   *gracilis* ....Slender "
Euonymus atropurpureus ....Burning Bush.
    "   *latifolius* ....Broad-leaved do.
Forsythia viridissima ....Golden Bell.
Halesia tetraptera ....Silver   "
Hibiscus Syriacus fl. pl ....Rose of Sharon, double.
Hydrangea paniculata grandiflora ....Great-panicled Hydrangea.
    "   *Hortensia* ....Common   "
    "   *Japonica* ....Japan   "
Kerria Japonica. ....Japan Globe-flower.
Lonicera Tartarica. ....Tartarian Honeysuckle.

Magnolia glauca .... Sweet Bay Magnolia.
"   *conspicua* .... Yulan Tree.
"   *Soulangeana*. .... Soulanges' Magnolia.
Philadelphus coronarius .... Mock Orange.
"   *nanus* .... "   "   Dwarf.
Ribes aureum .... Missouri Currant.
"   *Gordonianum* .... Gordon's   "
Syringa vulgaris .... Common Lilac.
"   "   *alba* .... White   "
"   *Persica*. .... Persian   "
"   "   *alba* .... "   "   White.
Spiræa prunifolia fl. pl .... Plum-leaved Spiræa.
"   *callosa and var. alba*. .... Flat-topped   "
"   *Reevesii fl. pl* .... Lance-leaved   "
"   *Douglasii* .... Douglas'   "
"   *hypericifolia* .... St. Peter's Wreath.
Viburnum Opulus.. .... Snowball.
"   *plicatum* .... Dwarf Snowball.
Weigela rosea .... Bush-Honeysuckle, Rose.
"   "   *fol. var* .... "   "   Variegated.
"   *nivea* .... "   "   White.
"   *amabalis* .... "   "   Lovely.
"   *Deboisianna* . ... "   "   Debois'.
Azalea Pontica, hybrids .... Belgian Azaleas.
Cercis Japonica .... Japan Judas Tree.
Pyrus Japonica .... Japan Quince.
Prunus triloba .... Flowering Plum.
Stuartia pentagynia .... Stuartia.
Symphoricarpus racemosus .... Snowberry.

HARDY EVERGREEN SHRUBS.

Andromeda floribunda .... Free-flowering Andomeda.
Buxus sempervirens arborea. .... Tree-Box.
Biota orientalis .... Eastern Arbor-Vitæ.
Cephalotaxus Fortunii ....
Daphne Cneorum .... Garland Flower.
Ilex opaca .... American Holly.
Juniperus communis var. Suecica .... Sweedish Juniper.
"   "   "   *Hibernica*.. .....Irish   "
"   *oblonga pendula* .... Weeping   "
"   *squamata* .... Scaled Juniper.
"   *prostrata* .... Prostrate   "
Kalmia latifolia .... American Laurel.
Podocarpus Japonica .... Japan Yew.
Retinispora obtusa .... Obtuse-leaved Retinispora.
"   *plumosa aurea* .... Golden-plumed   "
Rhododendron Catawbiense, hybrids..... Rhododrendons.

Taxus baccata, var. Canadensis.........American **Yew.**
"   "   " *erecta*..............Upright   "
Thuja occidentalis.....................American Arbor-vitæ.
"   " *var. Sibirica*...........Siberian   "   "
"   "   " *plicata*............Plicate   "   "
"   "   " *nana*.............Dwarf   "   "

HARDY EVERGREEN TREES OF MEDIUM SIZE.

Abies Canadensis.....................Hemlock Spruce.
"   " *var. Sargenti*..........Sargent's   "
" *excelsa*........................Norway   "
"   " *var. Gregoryana*...........Gregory's   "
"   "   " *pygmœa*..............Dwarf   "
"   "   " *inverta*..............Inverted   "
" *nigra pumila*....................Dwarf Black Spruce.
" *Fraseri var. Hudsonica*..........Hudson's Bay Fir.
" *pectinata*......................European Silver Fir.
"   " *var. fastigiata*...........Erect   "   "
" *Pichta*..........................Siberian   "   "
Juniperus Virginiana...................Red Cedar.
Pinus Strobus........................White Pine.
" *Cembra*.......................Swiss Stone **Pine.**
" *pumilio*........................Dwarf Pine.
" *Austriaca*......................Austrian "

HARDY CLIMBERS.

Ampelopsis quinquefolia................Virginia Creeper.
" *tricuspidata, (Vietchii)*.......Vietch's   "
Akebia quinata........................Akebia.
Aristolochia Sipho....................Dutchman's Pipe.
Bignonia grandiflora...................Large-flowered Trumpet vine
Clematis Flammula.....................Virgin's Bower.
" *Viticella*......................"   "
" *azurea*, and the various hybrids.
Hedera Helix..........................European Ivy.
This in its many varieties is scarcely hardy at New York.
Lonicera sempervirens..................Trumpet Honeysuckle.
" *Japonica*......................Japan   "
"   " *var. aurea*............Golden   "
" *Periclymenum*.................English Woodbine.
"   " *var. Belgica*......Dutch Honeysuckle.
" *Hallii*........................Hall's   "
Tecoma radicans.....................Trumpet Creeper.
Wistaria frutescens....................American Wistaria.
" *Sinensis*......................Chinese   "
"   " *var. alba*..............White   "
"   "   " *Allenii*...........Allen's   "
" *magnifica*.....................Magnificent   "

CHAPTER XXXIV

HARDY HERBACEOUS PERENNIALS.

Herbaceous perennials include those hardy plants, the stems of which die down at the approach of winter, or earlier if they have completed their growth ; the roots being hardy, they remain in the same place for several years in succession. Plants of this class were formerly more popular than they have been of late years, the taste for brilliant bedding effects having caused these former favorites to be neglected. Recently the taste for perennials has revived, and while they cannot serve as substitutes for what are known as bedding plants, they are exceedingly useful for those who wish to have flowers with but little trouble, as most of them can remain for three or four years without requiring any other care than to keep them clear of weeds. When the clumps become too large they require to be lifted, divided, and re-set in fresh soil. For the best results it is advisable to re-set most of them every third year, while some may remain in place indefinitely, taking care to give them a yearly manuring, as the vigorous growing ones soon exhaust the soil immediately around them. In setting out these plants, the taller growing kinds should be placed at the rear of the border, or in the center if the bed is to be seen from both sides, while those of the lowest growth are to be placed at the edge, and those of intermediate size are to be placed between. A proper selection of these plants will give a succession from early spring until frost stops all bloom. Many of these perennials are unchanged from their natural state, but bloom in our borders just as they appeared in their native woods and hills in different parts of the world, and seem to show no disposition to "break"

or deviate from their normal form, notwithstanding they
have been in cultivation for a century or two.   On the
other hand many have, by sporting, or by hybridizing,
and crossing, as in the case of pæonies, phloxes, irises,
and others, produced many florists varieties, which show
forms and colors not found in the native state of the
plants, and the frequent occurrence of double flowers
among them shows that cultivation has not been without
its influence.

With such a number to select from, it is difficult to
make a list of 25, or even 50, and not leave out many desirable kinds.   Those in the following list are all of generally admitted excellence, and are usually to be obtained
from florists and nurserymen.

It may be added here that there is no part of the country which does not afford wild flowers of sufficient beauty
to merit a place in the garden, and most of them, except
perhaps those which naturally grow in a deep shade, will
grow larger and bloom finer in a rich border than in their
native localities.

Perennials are propagated by division of the clumps,
by cuttings of the stems, and sometimes of the roots,
and by seeds.   In many cases the seeds are very slow of
germination unless sown as soon as ripe.   As most of
them do not bloom until the seedlings have made one
year's growth, the seeds should be sown in a reserve bed,
from which at the end of the first summer, or in the following spring, they may be transplanted to the place
where they are to flower.   It is well to give the seedlings
some protection the first winter, not because they are not
hardy, but to prevent them from being thrown out of the
soil by frequent freezing and thawing.   A covering of
evergreen boughs is most suitable, but if these are not at
hand, use coarse hay or other litter, first laying down
some brush, to keep the covering from matting down
upon them.

Aconitum Napellus....................Monkshood.
      "   *variegatum*.................Variegated Monkshood.
Anemone Japonica.....................Japan Windflower.
      "   var. *Honorine Jobert*..........White Japan   "
      "   *Pulsatilla* ....Pasque Flower.
Aquilegia alpina......................Alpine Columbine.
      "   *cærulea* ....Rocky Mt.   "
      "   *chrysantha* ....Golden-spurred Columbine.
      "   *vulgaris*......................Garden   "
Astilbe Japonica........................(Incorrectly Spiræa.)
Asperula odorata......................Woodruff.
Baptisia australis......................False Indigo.
Campanula Carpathica.................Carpathian Harebell.
      "   *persicifolia*...................Peach-leaved   "
      "   *grandiflora*...................Great-flowered "
   and others.
Cassia Marilandica....................Wild Senna.
Clematis erecta.........................Upright Clematis.
      "   *integrifolia*....................Entire-leaved "
Colchicum autumnale.................Meadow Saffron.
Convallaria majalis....................Lily of the Valley.
Delphinium elatum.....................Bee Larkspur.
      "   *nudicaule*...................Scarlet   "
   and others.
Dianthus plumarius....................Garden Pink.
      "   *superbus*.....................Fringed   "
Dicentra eximia......................Plumy Dicentra.
      "   *spectabilis*.....................Bleeding Heart.
Dictamnus Fraxinella.................Fraxinella.
Dodecatheon Meadia...................Am. Cowslip.
Eranthis hiemalis.....................Winter Aconite.
Erica carnea.........................Winter Heath.
Funkia ovata.........................Blue Day Lily.
      " *Japonica*.... ....Japan "   "
Gypsophila paniculata.................Panicled Gypsophila.
Helleborus niger......................Christmas Rose.
Hepatica triloba........................Liver-leaf.
      "   " *fl. pl.*...................Double do.
Iberis Gibraltarica....................Gibraltar Candytuft.
      "   *sempervirens*...................Perennial   "
Iris Germanica.......................German Flower de Luce.
   " *Iberica*.........................Iberian   "   " "
   " *pumila* ....Dwarf   "   " "
and many others of a great range of colors.
Liatris spicata........................Blazing Star.
      "   *squarrosa*................... .   "   "
   and others.

Lilium auratum ....Gold-banded Lily,
this, with many other Japanese species in the catalogues, is perfectly
hardy, and there should be a good collection of them in every garden.

Linum perenne ....Perennial Flax.

Lobelia cardinalis ....Cardinal Flower.
This native, (also its hybrids), does perfectly well in the drier soil of
the garden.

Lupinus polyphyllus ....Many-leaved Lupine.

Lychnis Chalcedonica ....Scarlet Lychnis,
    and several others.

Lysimachia nummularia ....Moneywort.

Mertensia Virginica ....Virginia Lungwort.

Myosotis palustris ....Forget-me-not.
    "   *Azorica* ....Azorian Forget-me-not.
    "   *dissitiflora* ....Early   "   "   "

Narcissus biflorus ....Primrose Peerless.
    "   *poeticus* ....Poet's Narcissus.
    "   *Jonquilla* ....Jonquil.
    "   *Pseudo-narcissus* ....Daffodil,
    in double and single varieties.

Œnothera Missouriensis ....Missouri Evening Primrose.

Pæonia officinalis ....Common Pæony,
and the various hydrids of this and other species, of which there are
many fine named sorts.

Pæonia tenuifolia ....Fennel-leaved Pæony.
    "   *Moutan* ....Tree   "
    of which there are many named varieties.

Papaver orientale ....Oriental Poppy.

Pentstemon grandiflorus ....Large-flowered Pentstemon.
    "   *barbatus var. Torreyi* ....Torrey's   "
    "   *Palmeri* ....Palmer's   "
    and several other hardy species.

Phlox, herbaceous ....French Lilac.
Under this head a great number of florists named varieties may be had.
New ones are offered every year, and a good selection of colors makes a
grand show.

Phlox subulata ....Moss Pink.
    Also the white variety.

Polemonium reptans ....Jacob's Ladder.
    "   *cæruleum* ....Greek Valerian.

Primula veris ....Eng. Cowslip.
This and the Polyanthus varieties need a moist and shady place. *P.
cortusoides* is hardy, and *P. Japonica* probably so.

Pyrethrum carneum ....Rosy Pyrethrum,
    the new double varieties.

Saxifraga crassifolia ....Thick-leaved Saxifrage.
    "   *cordifolia* ....Heart-leaved   "

Sedum acre...........................Stone crop.
 " *Sieboldii* (and var.)..............Siebold's Stone crop.
 " *pulchellum*.....................Beautiful " "
 " *spectabile*.......................Showy " "
and a large number of others, presenting a great variety in foliage and flowers.

Sempervivum arachnoideum.............Cobweb Houseleek.
 " *calcaratum*.................Purple-tipped "
 " *tectorum*.................. Common "

Of these curious plants there are more than 50 species in cultivation, and all perfectly hardy ; useful on rock-work.

Spiræa filipendula, (and double)........Dropwort.
 " *palmata*........................Palmate Spiræa.
 " *Ulmaria* ....Queen of the Meadow.
 " *venusta* ....Queen of the Prairie.
Symphytum officinale var...............Variegated Comfrey.
Thalictrum minus......................Maiden-hair Meadow Rue.
Tritoma uvaria, (and vars.).............Red-hot Poker,
needs covering in winter with litter.
Tunica Saxifraga ....Rock Tunica.
Yucca filamentosa..... ....Bear-Grass.

PERENNIAL ORNAMENTAL GRASSES.

1. *Arundo Donax*.........................Great Reed.
2. " " *versicolor*............. ...Variegated Reed.
3. " *conspicua*....................Silvery "
4. *Erianthus Ravennæ*...................Ravenna grass.
5. *Eulalia Japonica var*..................Japan Eulalia.
6. *Festuca glauca*... ....Blue Fescue.
7. *Gynerium argenteum*..................Pampas grass.
8. *Panicum virgatum*....................Wand-like Panic.
9. *Phalaris arundinacea picta*............Ribbon grass.
10. *Stipa pennata*........................Feather grass.

In the climate of New York, Nos. 1, 2 and 7 need protection ; Nos. 1 and 2 by litter over the roots, and No. 7 by covering it with a cask or box. In the order of their hight, No. 6 is 6 inches, 9 and 10 a foot, 5 and 8, 3 to 4 feet, and 1, 2, 3, 4, and 7 from 6 to 12 feet, according to the age of the plants.

CHAPTER XXXV.

ANNUAL FLOWERING PLANTS.

To make a selection from the bewildering number of varieties now offered in our seed catalogues, is an interesting, though it may be sometimes rather a perplexing operation. It is not very easy to give specific advice in the matter, as tastes are so varied. We would say, in general terms though, be shy of "novelties" until you see them recommended in the lists the second year ; you may then know that their merits have been tested and they are given permanent place. We have been importers of all such "novelties" for over twenty years, and think ourselves lucky if we get one good thing for every nineteen worthless ones we try. Still, to get the good things, all that are offered must be tried, and subjected to the sifting process—separating the chaff from the wheat. We can only use space to enumerate a few generally favorite kinds, which we give in the list below; this comprises such as are of easiest cultivation, and are most valued for the beauty or fragrance of their flowers.

Asters,	Escholtzia,	Nasturtiums,
Balsams,	Geraniums,	Nemophila,
Candytufts,	Globe Amaranths,	Pansy,
Cannas,	Helichrysums,	Petunia,
*Canary Bird Flower,	Ice Plant,	Phlox Drummondii,
Carnations,	*Ipomæa,	Poppy,
Clarkias,	Lobelia,	Portulaca,
Cockscombs,	Lupines,	Scabiosa,
Collinsia,	Lychnis,	Schizanthus,
*Convolvulus,	Marigolds,	*Sweet Peas,
*Cypress Vine,	Mignonnette,	Stocks,
Delphiniums,(Larkspur)	Mimosa,(Sensitive-plant)	Zinnias,
Dianthus,		

Those Marked * are climbers.

I have used the popular and scientific names indiscriminately in the way they are given in most seed catalogues, as this will facilitate reference to them for descriptions. The rule for the sowing of seeds already given in the chapter " Propagation of Plants by Seeds," applies to sowing the seeds of annuals whether in the hotbed or greenhouse, to obtain plants to set in the open border, or sowing at once in the open border. The covering of the seeds should in every case be of a light material. Thus, if the soil of your flower-garden is hard and rough, be sure that the surface on which the delicate seeds are to be sown is made smooth and level, and that it is covered with a fine light soil, such as leaf-mold, in the manner described in the chapter referred to. Probably three-fourths of all the flower-seeds that are sown by amateurs never germinate, and for no other reason than that they have not been properly treated. One sows a tropical seed, such as Portulaca, in March, and wonders that it does not start to grow; by May, the time it should be sown in the ground, the spot has become covered with weeds, and the tiny plant, if it comes now at all, is choked and killed. Another reverses the order and wonders that the hardy Pansy seeds which are sown in June, fail to grow, or if they grow, fail to bloom in the dog days. Our seed catalogues are nearly all defective in not giving more specific directions for the culture of annual plants ; if the space used for description of form and color was devoted to telling the time and manner of sowing, it would be of far more benefit to the amateur buyer, but nearly all follow the English practice of giving descriptions of varieties only. There the necessity for such information is less, the people being better informed as to flower culture, and the climate is also more congenial for germination of most seeds.

CHAPTER XXXVI.

FLOWERS WHICH WILL GROW IN THE SHADE.

There are few plants that will flower in places from which sunshine is entirely excluded. Some plants will grow well enough, developing shoots and leaves, but *flowers* of nearly all kinds must have some sunshine. Of those that do well and flower when planted out in the open ground where sunlight only comes for two or three hours during the day, may be named the following: Calceolarias, Fuchsias, Lobelias, Herbaceous Phloxes, Pansies, Forget-me-nots, Lily of the Valley, and other herbaceous plants and shrubs whose native habitat is shady woods. Perhaps a better effect is produced in such situations by ornamental leaved plants, such as Coleuses of all kinds, Amaranths, Achyranthes, Caladiums, Cannas, and other plants with high colored or ornamental leaves. With these may be combined the different styles of white or gray-leaved plants, such as Centaureas, Cinerarias, Gnaphaliums—plants known under the general popular term of "Dusty Millers." For our own part we much prefer to devote shaded situations to such plants, rather than to see the abortive attempts to produce flowers made by plants in positions where there is no sunshine. It may be here remarked that the cultivator of plants in rooms should understand the necessity of sunlight to plants that are to flower, and endeavor to get them as near as possible to a window having an eastern or a southern aspect. The higher the temperature, the more plants suffer for the want of light. Many plants, such as Geraniums, Fuchsias, or Roses, might remain in a temperature of 40 degrees, in a cellar for example, away from direct light for months without material injury, while if the cellar contained a furnace keeping up a temperature of 70 degrees, they would all die before the winter was ended, particularly if the plants were of a half hardy nature. If tropical species, they might stand it better, but all plants quickly become enfeebled when kept at high temperature and away from the light.

CHAPTER XXXVII.

INSECTS.

When insects attack plants in the greenhouse, parlor, or anywhere under cover, we can generally manage to get them under control, but when they attack plants in the open air, it is according to our experience, difficult to destroy them. Insects are injurious to plants in the open air in two principal ways : some attack the branches and leaves, and others infest the roots. When insects attack the roots of a plant, we have been able to do but little to stop their ravages. We can manage somewhat better with those attacking the leaves, but even this division of the enemy is often too much for us. As a preventive, we would strongly advise that birds of all kinds should be encouraged. Since the European sparrows have favored us with their presence in such numbers, insects of nearly all kinds have much decreased. Most people will remember the disgusting " measuring worm " that festooned the shade-trees in New York, Brooklyn, and other cities ten years ago ; these made their exit almost in proportion to the increase of sparrows, and now hardly one is to be seen. The same is true of the Rose slug. In my rose grounds, a few years ago, we were obliged to employ a number of boys for weeks during the summer to shake off and kill the Rose slug in order to keep the plants alive, but since we have had the sparrows in such numbers, hardly one of these pests is now seen. An examination of the crop of a sparrow killed in July, showed that it contained Rose slugs, Aphis, or green-fly, and the seeds of chickweed and other plants, proving beyond question the fact that they are promiscuous feeders. The Rose slug, (*Selandria rosæ*), referred to above, is a light green, soft insect, varying from $\frac{1}{16}$ of an inch to nearly an inch in length. There are apparently two species or varieties, one of which eats only the cuticle of the lower side of the leaf, the other eats it entire. The first is by far the most destructive here. In a few days after the plants are attacked they appear as if they had been burned. An excellent application for the *prevention* of the ravages of the Rose slug is whale-oil soap dissolved in the proportion of one lb. to eight gallons of water, this, if steadily applied daily for a week with a syringe on Rose plants, before the leaf has developed in spring, will entirely prevent the attacks of the insect. But we find that if the slug once gets fairly at work, this remedy is powerless unless used so strong as to injure the leaves.

The Rose-Bug, (*Macrodactylus subspinosus*), or Rose Chaffer, gets its name from the preference it shows for the buds and blossoms of the Rose, though it is equally destructive to the Dahlia, Aster, Balsam, and many other flowers, and especially grape blossoms. All the ordinary remedies seem to fail with the Rose-bug, and it can only be stopped by picking it off by hand.

Green-Fly, or *Aphis*, is one of the most common, but fortunately most easily destroyed, of any insect that infests plants, either in-doors or out. In our greenhouses, as already stated, we fumigate twice a week, by burning about half a pound of refuse tobacco stems, (made damp), to every 500 square feet of glass surface, but in private greenhouses or on plants in rooms, fumigating is often impracticable. Then the tobacco stems can be used by steeping one pound in five gallons of water, until the water gets to be the color of strong tea. This liquid applied over and under the leaves with a syringe, will destroy the insect quite as well as by fumigating, only in either case the application should be made before the insects are seen, to prevent their coming rather than to destroy them when established; for often by neglect they get a foothold in such legions that all remedies become ineffectual to dislodge them. Another means of preventing the green-fly is to apply tobacco in the shape of dust. The sweepings of tobacco warehouses, which can be found for sale in most seed or agricultural establishments, at a cost of five to ten cents per pound. This applied once or twice a week to an ordinary sized private greenhouse, would effectually prevent any injury from green-fly. No special quantity of this need be prescribed, all that is necessary is to see that it is so dusted on that it reaches all parts of the plant and on both sides of the leaves. It is best to slightly syringe the plants beforehand, so that the dust will adhere to the leaves. When applied to plants out-doors, it should be done in the morning when the dew is on. Fruit-trees of many kinds, shrubs, and Roses of all kinds, out of doors, are particularly liable to injury from some species of Aphis, but the application of tobacco dust, if made in time, will be found a cheap and effectual remedy.

Ground or Blue Aphis, is a close relative of the preceeding, but it gets its living from the roots down in the soil, while the Green Aphis feeds in the air on the leaves. The Blue Aphis attacks a great many varieties of plants, particularly in hot, dry weather, and whenever Asters, Verbenas, Petunias, Centaureas, or such plants begin to droop, it will be found on examination, in three cases out of four, that the farthest extremities of their roots are completely surrounded by the Blue Aphis. The only remedy we have ever found for this pest is a strong de-

coction of tobacco, made so strong as to resemble strong
coffee in color. The earth around the plants must be
soaked with this so that the lowest roots will be reached.
The tobacco water will not hurt the plants, but will be
fatal to the insect, and if it has not already damaged the
roots to too great an extent, may prove a remedy.

Ants.—These are not usually troublesome unless in
great numbers, yet when they appear in strong force they
are often very destructive. About the simplest method
we have found to get rid of them, is to lay fresh bones
around the infested plants ; they will leave everything
to feed on these, and when thus accumulated may be
easily destroyed.

The Red Spider is one of the most insidious enemies
of plants, both when under glass and in the open air in
summer. It luxuriates in a hot and dry atmosphere,
and the only remedy that I can safely recommend to amateurs, is copious syringings with water, if in the greenhouse, so that a moist atmosphere can be obtained. This,
of course, is not practicable when plants are grown in
rooms, and the only thing that can then be done is to
sponge off the leaves. It is this insect, more than any
thing else, that makes it so difficult to grow plants in the
dry air of the sitting-room, as it may be sapping the
life blood from a plant, and its owner never discover the
cause of his trouble. It is so minute as hardly to be
seen by the naked eye, but its ravages soon show, and if
the leaves of your plants begin to get brown, an examination of the under-surface of the leaf will usually reveal
the little pests in great numbers. When they get thus
established there is no remedy but to sponge the leaves
thoroughly with water, or weak soapsuds.

The Mealy Bug, as it is generally called, is a white
mealy or downy-looking insect, which is often very troublesome among hot-house plants, but rarely does any
harm amongst those that can live in a cool room, as no

doubt it is a native of some tropical country, and can only exist in such a temperature as is required by plants of that kind. There are various remedies used by florists, but the use of nearly all of them might do more harm than good in inexperienced hands, and I therefore advise that they should only be destroyed by being washed off such plants as Gardenias, or rubbed off of more tender leaved plants with a soft brush ; or where there are but few, they may be readily picked off by the use of a quill sharpened like a toothpick.

Brown and White Scale Insects.—These appear lifeless, and adhere closely to the stems of such plants as Oleanders, Ivies, etc., and like the Mealy Bug are best destroyed by being washed or rubbed off.

Thrips.—This is an insect varying in color from light yellow to dark brown, and much more active in its movements than the Green-Fly, and more difficult to destroy ; when it once gets a foothold it is very destructive. It succumbs to tobacco, in any of the forms recommended for the destruction of Green-Fly, but not so readily. It luxuriates in shaded situations, and generally abounds where plants are standing too thickly together, or where ventilation or light is deficient. It may be safely asserted that in any well regulated place where plants are kept, no injury from insects will ever become serious if due attention has been given to keeping the atmosphere of the place moist, and using tobacco freely in any of the forms we have recommended.

The Angle Worm.—This is the common worm seen in every soil in pots and in the open ground. It is harmless so far as feeding goes, for it seems never to touch plants as food, but it bores and crawls around in a way by no means beneficial to pot-grown plants ; it is, however, easily dislodged ; by slaking a quart of lime and adding water to make up ten gallons of the liquid, and watering the plants with it after it has become clear, the caustic qualities of the lime will be quickly fatal to the worm.

———◦◦———

CHAPTER XXXVIII.

MILDEW.

Mildew is a parasitical fungus, often seen on greenhouse and other plants, and is quickly destructive to their health. But as with all other plant troubles, it is best to prevent rather than cure. Care should be taken, particularly where roses or grape vines are grown under glass, as both of these are especially liable to be attacked, to avoid a rapid change of temperature, or a long exposure to sudden chill by draughts in ventilating. As soon as spots of grayish-white appear on the leaves of roses or grape-vines, either out-doors or under glass, it is certain that mildew is present, but if it has not been neglected too long, the following preparation will usually be found a prompt remedy. Take three pounds each of flowers of sulphur and quick-lime, put together and slake the lime, and add six gallons of water ; boil all together until it is reduced to two gallons, allow the liquid to settle until it gets clear, then bottle for use. One gill only of this is to be mixed in five gallons of water, and syringed over the plants in the evening, taking care not to use it on the fruit when ripe, as it would communicate a taste and smell which would render it useless. Applied in this weak state, it does not injure the leaves, and yet has the power to destroy the low form of vegetable growth, which we call mildew. We apply it just as we do tobacco, once or twice a week, as a preventive, and we rarely have a speck of mildew.

CHAPTER XXXIX.

FROZEN PLANTS.

When by any mishap the plants, whether in parlor or greenhouse, become frozen, either at once remove them, (taking care not to touch the leaves), to some place warm enough to be just above the point of freezing ; if there are too many to do that, get up the fire as rapidly as possible and raise the temperature. The usual advice is to sprinkle the leaves and shade the plants from the sun. We have never found either remedy of any avail with frozen plants, and the sprinkling is often a serious injury if done before the temperature is above the freezing point. In our experience with thousands of frozen plants, we have tried all manner of expedients, and found no better method than to get them out of the freezing atmosphere as quickly as possible, and we have also found that the damage is in proportion to the succulent condition of the plant, and the intensity of the freezing. Just what degree of cold plants in any given condition can endure without injury, we are unable to state. Plants are often frozen so that the leaves hang down, but when thawed out are found to be not at all injured ; at another time the same low temperature acting on the same kind of plants may kill them outright if they happen to be growing more thriftily, and are full of sap. When the frost is penetrating into a greenhouse or room in which plants are kept, and the heating arrangements are inadequate to keep it out, the best thing to do is to cover the plants with paper, (newspapers), or sheeting ; thus protected, most plants will be enabled to resist four or five degrees of frost ; paper is rather better than sheeting for this purpose.

6

CHAPTER XL.

MULCHING.

Litter of any kind placed around newly planted trees to prevent evaporation from the soil, was the original meaning of mulch, but it is at present extended to include a covering of the soil applied at any time, and for very different purposes. Good cultivators apply hay, straw, or other litter to the surface of the soil to protect the roots of certain plants against the action of frost, it being useful, not so much against freezing as to prevent the alternate freezing and thawing, that is apt to occur in our variable and uncertain climate, even in mid-winter. As mentioned under strawberry culture, the mulch applied in the fall protects the roots during winter, it is allowed to remain on the bed where, if thick enough, it keeps down weeds, and prevents the evaporation of moisture from the soil during the dry time we are apt to have between the flowering and the ripening of the strawberry. Besides all this, it makes a clean bed for the fruit to rest upon, and should a driving shower come up as the fruit is ripening, there is no danger that the berries will be splashed with mud and spoiled. The utility of a mulch is not confined to the strawberry among fruits ; raspberries and currants are much benefitted by it, and by its use a gardener of my acquaintance succeeds in growing fine crops of the fine varieties of English gooseberries, a fruit with which very few succeed in our hot summers. Newly planted trees, whether of fruit or ornamental kinds, are much benefitted by a mulch, and its application often settles the question of success or failure. We have known a whole pear orchard to be mulched, and the owner thought its cost was more than repaid by saving the fallen fruit from bruises. The rooting of a layer is by some gardeners thought to be facilitated by placing a flat stone over the buried branch; the fact being that the stone acts as a mulch, and prevents the soil around the cut portion from drying out, and greatly favors the rooting process. Even in the vegetable garden, mulching is found useful, especially with cauliflowers, which find our summers quite too dry. The material of the mulch is not of much importance, the effect being purely mechanical, one kind of litter will answer as well as another; the material will be governed in great measure by locality; those living near salt water will find salt-hay, as hay from the marshes is called, the most readily procured; those who live near pine forests use the fallen leaves, or pine needles as they are called; in the grain growing districts straw is abundant, and nothing can be better; it can be applied more thoroughly if run through a cutter, though the thrashing machine often makes it short enough. Leaves are nature's own mulch, and answer admirably; if there is danger of their being blown away, brush laid over them, or even a little earth sprinkled on them will keep them in place. Tan-bark and sawdust may serve for some uses, but they are very bad for strawberries, their finer particles being about as objectionable as the soil. One of the best materials to use for summer mulching is the green grass mowed from lawns. This applied to the thickness of two or three inches around the roots of all kinds of small fruits, will be found not only to greatly benefit the crop, particularly in dry weather, but will save greatly in labor by preventing the growth of weeds. One of our best private gardeners in the vicinity of New York has adopted this summer mulching with the grass from the lawn for nearly twenty years, and has succeeded in growing all kinds of small fruits in the highest degree of perfection.

CHAPTER XLI.

ARE PLANTS IN ROOMS INJURIOUS TO HEALTH?

The question whether plants may be safely grown in living rooms is now settled by scientific men, who show that whatever deleterious gases may be given out by plants at night they are so minute in quantity that no injury is ever done by their presence in the rooms and by being inhaled. Though we were glad to see the question disposed of by such authority, experience had already shown that no bad effects ever resulted from living in apartments where plants were grown. Our greenhouses are one mass of foliage, and I much doubt if any healthier class of men can be found than those engaged in the care of plants. But timid persons may say that the deleterious gases are given out only at night, while our greenhouse operatives are only employed in daylight. This is only true in part. Our watchmen and men engaged in attending to fires at night make the warm greenhouses their sitting-room and their sleeping-room, and I have yet to hear of the first instance where the slightest injury resulted from this practice. Many of our medical practitioners run in old ruts. Some Solomon among them probably gave out this dogma a century ago, it was made the convenient scape-goat of some other cause of sickness, and the rank and file have followed in his train. A belief in this error often consigns to the cellar, or to the cold winds of winter, the treasured floral pets of a household.

CHAPTER XLII.

SHADING.

In mulching the object is to prevent evaporation from the soil, as well as to shield the roots from sudden changes of temperature ; it is often necessary to protect the whole plant in this respect, and this is accomplished by shading. Although on a large scale, we can do little in the way of shading plants in the open ground, yet the amateur will often find it of great utility, as screening will frequently save a recently transplanted plant, which without it would be quite ruined by a few hours' exposure to the sun. For shading small plants in the border, such as transplanted annuals, a few shingles will be found very useful, one or two of these can be stuck in the ground so as to completely protect the delicate plant and yet not deprive it of air. Six-inch boards of half-inch stuff nailed together to form a V shaped trough are very useful in the garden ; they are handy to place over small plants during cold nights, and may be turned over and set to make a screen against strong winds, or used for shading plants in rows. Seedlings often suffer from the heat of the sun in the middle of the day ; the seedlings of even the hardiest forest trees are very delicate when young. The seeds of such trees when sown naturally almost always fall where the young plant will be shaded, and the amateur who experiments in this very interesting branch of horticulture, the raising of evergreen and deciduous trees and shrubs from seed, will find it necessary to imitate nature and protect his young seedlings from the intense heat of the sun. There are several ways of doing this ; if the seeds have been sown in an open border, let him take twigs about a foot long, evergreen if they can be had, but if not, those from any deciduous tree, and stick them a few inches apart all over the bed. This will give the seedlings very much such a protection as they would naturally have had in the shade of other plants, and though evergreens will look better for a while, the dead leaves of deciduous twigs will give quite as useful a shade. It is always safer to sow seeds in a frame, as the young plants are then under more complete control. Frames are easily shaded by means of a lattice made of common laths. Strips of inch stuff an inch and a half or two inches wide, are used for the sides of the lattice, and laths are nailed across as far apart as their own width. One lath being nailed on, another is laid down to mark the distance, the third one put down and nailed, and the second lath is moved along to mark the distance for the fourth, and so on. With a screen of this kind there is abundant light, but the sun does not shine long at a time on one spot, and the plants have a constantly changing sun and shade. This lath screen may be used for shading plants in the open ground if supported at a proper hight above them. In a propagating house, where it is necessary, as it often is, to shade cuttings, a lattice laid upon the outside of the glass answers a good purpose. The laths are sometimes tied together with strong twine, the cord answering the place of slats, and serving as a warp with which the laths are woven; the advantage of a screen of this kind is that it can be rolled up. Plants kept in windows during the summer months will, if in a sunny exposure, require some kind of a shade, and if the one provided to keep the sun from the room shuts out too much light, or excludes air as well as sun, something must be provided which will give protection during the heat of the day, and still allow sufficient light and an abundant circulation of air. Any one with ingenuity can arrange a screen of white cotton cloth to answer the purpose.

The old practice of stripping the greenhouse in summer is falling into disuse, and by a proper selection of plants and sufficient shade, it is made as attractive then as at any other season, but even for tropical plants the glass must be shaded. For a small lean-to, a screen of light canvass or muslin arranged upon the outside, so that it may be wound up on a roller when not wanted will answer, and if it be desired to keep the house as cool as possible, this should be so contrived that there will be a space of six inches or so between that and the glass. But upon a large house, or one with a curvilinear roof, this is not so manageable, and the usual method is to coat the glass with some material which will obstruct a part of the light. The most common method is to give the outside of the glass a coat of ordinary lime whitewash ; this makes a sufficient shade, and is gradually dissolved by the rains, so that by autumn the coating is removed, or so nearly so that what remains may be readily washed off. A more pleasant effect is produced by spattering the glass with the same wash, which can be done by a dexterous use of the brush and flirting it so as to leave the wash in numerous fine drops, like rain-drops. Others use whiting and milk for the same purpose. Whatever may be the means of effecting it, we find that in this latitude shading of some kind is required from about the 1st of May to the middle of September by nearly all plants grown under glass. Ferns, Lycopods, Caladiums, Primulas, Fuchsias, Begonias, Gloxinias, Achimenes, Lobelias, Smilax, and plants of that character require the glass to be heavily shaded, while for Roses, Carnations, Bouvardias, Poinsettias, Geraniums of all kinds, and nearly all succulent plants, do not need so much. The method of spattering the glass outside with thin whitewash, allows the shading to be light or heavy, as required. When first done, it is spattered very thinly, merely to break the strong glare of the sun, just about thick enough to half

cover the surface. As the season advances, the spattering should be repeated to increase the shade, but at no
time for the plants last mentioned do we entirely cover
the glass.   In England, especially for fern houses,
Brunswick green mixed with milk is used, to give a
green shade, which is thought to be best suited to these
plants.   The blue glass for greenhouses which was so
highly lauded a few years ago, has not met with much
favor, but recent experiments in glazing with ground
glass have given such results as to warrant a more careful
investigation into the use of this material.

CHAPTER XLIII.

THE LAW OF COLOR IN FLOWERS.

I refer to this matter in the hope that it may be the
means of saving some of my readers, not only from being
duped and swindled, by a class of itinerant scamps that
annually reap a rich harvest in disposing of impossibili-
ties in flowers, but that I may assure them of the utter
improbability of their ever seeing such wonders as these
fellows offer, thereby saving them from parting with
money for worthless objects, and from the ridicule of
their friends who are already better advised.   This subject cannot be too often brought before our amateur horticulturists.   Warnings are given year after year in leading agricultural and other journals devoted to gardening,
yet a new crop of dupes is always coming up who readily
fall victims to the scoundrels who live upon their credu-
lity.   Not a season passes but some of these swindling
dealers have the audacity to plant themselves right in

the business centers of our large cities, and hundreds of our sharp business men glide smoothly into their nets. The very men who will chuckle at the misfortunes of a poor rustic when he falls into the hands of a mock auctioneer, or a pocket-book dropper, will freely pay $10 for a rose plant of which a picture has been shown them as having a blue flower ; the chance of its coming blue being about equal to the chance that the watch of the mock auctioneer will be gold. It has long been known among the best observers of such matters, that in certain families of plants, particular colors prevail, and that in no single instance can we ever expect to see *blue, yellow, and scarlet colors in varieties of the same species.* If any one at all conversant with plants will bring any family of them to mind, it will at once be seen how undeviating is this law. In the Dahlia we have scarlet and yellow, but no approach to blue, so in the Rose, Hollyhock, etc. Again in the Verbena, Salvia, etc., we have scarlet and blue, but no *yellow!* If we reflect it will be seen that there is nothing out of the order of nature in this arrange- ment. We never expect to see among our poultry with their varied but somber plumage, any assume the azure hues of our spring Blue-bird, or the dazzling tints of the Oriole ; why then should we expect nature to step out of what seems her fixed laws, and give us a blue Rose, a blue Dahlia, or a yellow Verbena ?

THE FRUIT GARDEN.

CHAPTER XLIV.

PRUNING.

Though the chapter on pruning is placed at the commencement of that division of the work which treats upon fruits, the fact must not be lost sight of that pruning is often quite as necessary upon trees and shrubs cultivated for their flowers or foliage as upon those grown for their fruit. In pruning we cut away some portion of a tree, shrub, or other plant, for the benefit of that which remains, and whether performed upon a branch six inches through, or upon a shoot so tender as to be cut by the thumb-nail, is essentially the same. The operation, though very simple, is one which the amateur often fears to undertake, and having no confidence in his own ability, he often employs some jobbing gardener, who has no fears on this or any other gardening matter. Pruning is done for various ends, and unless one has a definite reason for doing it, he had better leave it undone : Many have an idea that pruning must, for some reason, be done every year, just as it used to be thought necessary for people to be bled every spring, whether well or ill. We prune to control the shape of a tree or shrub, and by directing the growth from one part to another, obtain a symmetrical form, especially in fruit trees, where it is desirable that the weight of fruit be equally distributed. In some trees where the fruit is grown only on the wood of the previous season, the bearing portions are each year removed further and further from the body of the tree ; in such cases a shortening of the growth each year will cause the formation of a compact head instead of the loose straggling that results when this is omitted. We prune to renew the vigor of a plant ; the inexperienced cannot understand how cutting away a third, a half, or even more of a plant can improve it in vigor and fruitfulness, or abundance and size of flowers. Let us suppose that a stem which grew last year has 20 buds upon it; if this is allowed to take its own course in the spring, a few of the upper buds will push with great vigor, and form strong shoots; those below will make gradually weaker shoots, and for probably the lower third of the stem the buds will not start at all; the most vigorous growth is always at the top, the buds there were the last formed in the previous summer, are the most excitable, and the soonest to grow the next spring, and getting the start of those below them, they draw the nourishment to themselves and starve the others. If, instead of allowing this stem to grow at will in this manner, it had been, before any of the buds started, cut back to leave only a few of the lower ones, those having an abundance of nutriment would push forth with great vigor and be nearly equal in size, while the flowers or fruit borne upon them would be greatly superior to those upon the unpruned stem. Any one can readily be convinced of the utility of pruning by taking two rose-bushes of equal size, leaving one without any pruning to take care of itself, and each spring cutting the other back severely, pruning away one-third or one-half of the wood that was formed the previous season. The result at the end of two years will be very striking. No general rule can be given for pruning ; the amateur should use his eyes, and notice the habit of growth of his trees and shrubs. He will find that many, like the rose, produce their flowers upon the new wood of the present season, and that such plants are greatly benefitted by cutting back more or less each spring. But there are other plants for which this treatment will not answer ; if we examine a horse-chestnut-tree, or a lilac-bush, and many others, we shall find that the flowers come from the large buds that were formed on the end of last season's growth, and that to cut back such plants would be to remove all the flower-buds. With shrubs of this kind, all that need be done is to thin out the branches where they are too crowded. These examples will warn the novice against indiscriminate pruning, and unless as he stands before his shrub or tree, knife in hand, he knows why he is to prune and how, let him put his knife in his pocket, and give the plant the benefit of the doubt. While under the different fruits we can give directions for the particular pruning required by each, the proper method of treating a miscellaneous collection of ornamental shrubs and trees can only be learned by observation. The term pruning is generally applied to the cutting away, in whole or in part, of the ripened wood, but much pruning may be done by the use of the thumb and finger; this is termed pinching, and is practiced upon young shoots while they are yet soft. This most useful form of pruning allows us to control the form of a plant with the greatest ease, and is applied not only to soft-wooded plants, but to trees and shrubs, and may be so performed on these as to render nearly, if not quite, all pruning of ripened wood unnecessary. If a vigorous shoot has its end or "growing point" pinched out it will cease to elongate, but will throw out branches below, the growth of which may be controlled in the same manner; the blackberry illustrates the utility of this kind of pruning; the rampant growing shoot which springs up from the root will, if left to itself, make a long cane six or eight feet high, and with a very few branches near the top; if when this shoot has reached four, or at most five feet, its end be pinched off, it will then throw out numerous branches, and if the upper branches, when they reach the length of 18 inches, be "stopped," (as it is called), in a similar manner, by pinching, the growth will be directed to the lower ones, and by the end of the season instead of a long, unmanageable wand, there will be a well-

branched bush which will bear its fruit all within reach.
The grower of plants in pots is usually afraid to remove
even a single inch of the stem, and the result is usually
a lot of "leggy" specimens not worth the care that is
otherwise bestowed upon them.   Plants may be prevented
from ever reaching this condition, if their growth be
properly controlled by pinching ; but if they have once
reached it, they should be cut back severely, and a compact bushy form obtained from the new shoots which will
soon start.   The mechanical part of pruning is very simple, a sharp knife is the best implement, as it makes a
clean cut, without bruising
the bark, and the wound
quickly heals ; but shears are
much easier to handle, and
the work can be done so
much more quickly, that they
are generally preferred, and
for rampant growing bushes
will answer, but upon fruit-
trees, and choice plants generally, the knife is to be preferred.   The cut should be
made just at a joint; not so
far above it as to leave a

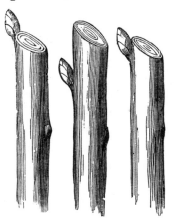

Fig. 48.   Fig. 49.   Fig. 50.
WHERE TO CUT IN PRUNING.

stub, as in fig. 49, which will die back to the bud, there
being nothing to contribute to its growth ; nor should it
be made so close to the bud as to endanger it, as in fig.
48 ; the cut should start just opposite the lower part of
the bud and end just above its top, as in fig. 50.   For
the removal of branches too large to cut with the knife,
as must sometimes be done on neglected trees, a saw is
required.   Saws are made especially for the purpose, but
any narrow one with the teeth set wide will answer ; the
rough cut left by the saw should be pared smooth, and if
an inch or more in diameter, the wound should be cov-

ered ; ordinary paint, melted grafting wax, or shellac
varnish will answer to protect the bare wood from air and
moisture, and prevent decay.

In pruning it is well to remember that the future
shape of the tree will be materially affected by the
position upon the branch of the bud to which the
cut is made ; the upper bud left on the branch will
continue the growth, and the new shoot will be in the
direction of that bud. If
a young tree is, as in fig.
51, to have all its branches
shortened, and each is cut
to a bud, A, pointing to-
wards the center of the tree,
the tendency of the new
growth will all be inward,
as in fig. 52 ; while if all
be cut to an outside bud,
B, the result will be to
spread the growth, as in
fig. 53. As to the time of
pruning, about which there
has been much discussion,
it may be done on small
stems at any time after the

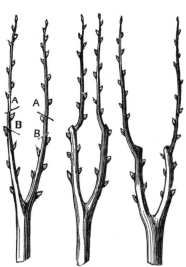

Fig. 51.   Fig. 52.   Fig. 53.
PRUNING FOR SHAPE.

fall of the leaf, before the growth starts in the spring,
but for the removal of large branches, late in winter is
regarded as the best time. Pinching is of course done
whenever it is needed.

CHAPTER XLV.

HARDY GRAPES.

Grapes can be grown in almost any soil, provided it is not a wet one, although the grape will take abundance of water when in a growing state, it must pass off quickly, else the growth will be impeded. If the ground is not naturally suitable, (*i. e.*, at least a foot in depth of good soil), a border prepared in the manner recommended in the chapter on "Cold Grapery," will well repay the trouble. It is imperative that the position where the vine is planted be such as will enable it to get sunlight for the greater portion of the day. Ten years ago I planted an arbor with an arched top and 100 feet long by 16 feet wide and 10 feet high, covering a walk running east and west; this gave a south and north exposure. The crop has always been excellent and abundant on the south side, and top of the arbor, but on the north side, (unless the first and second years of fruiting, when there was not sufficient foliage to impede the light), it has been nearly a failure. There is much misconception as to what should be the age of a grape-vine when planted; nine-tenths of our amateur customers ask for vines three or four years old. If a vine of that age could be properly lifted with every root unbroken, then there might be some advantage in its greater strength, but as vines are usually grown in the nurseries closely together, with the roots all interlaced, large plants can rarely be got with roots enough to support the vine and maintain its vigor after transplanting. As a rule it is better to plant one or two-year-old vines, which can usually be bought at half the price of those of three or four years old, and which in all probability will give a crop quite as soon, if not sooner, than the large ones. The manner of planting the vine is similar to that of setting any other tree or shrub. The ground must be thoroughly broken up, not in a mere hole only sufficient to hold the roots, but if a regular border has not been made, the place where each vine is to be planted, should not be less than three feet in diameter, and if double that, all the better, and to the depth of not less than a foot. On receiving the vine from the nursery, it may consist of one or more shoots,

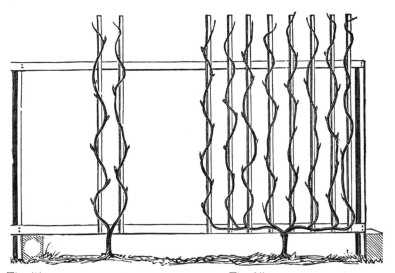

Fig. 54.—VINE WITH TWO SHOOTS.   Fig. 55.—VINE WITH ARMS.

but on planting it should be cut back to only two or three eyes or buds. On starting to grow, all of these buds or eyes should be rubbed off except one, selecting the strongest. Train this shoot perpendicularly to a stake the first year of its growth, the next fall, when the leaves drop, cut it back to nine or ten inches from the ground. When the vine starts the next spring, rub off all eyes or buds except two, which during the season will form two canes, as in fig. 54. These, if they are canes half an inch in diameter, are in fall to be pruned to three or four feet long, and the following spring are to be trained horizontally, one to the right, the other to the left. If at the end of the second year they are still small, it is better to delay laying down the arms until another year, and grow two upright shoots again, to get them sufficiently strong. These will form the base from which to start the upright shoots, as shown in fig. 55. These upright growths will be the permanent fruiting canes, and should be from 15 to 18 inches apart, and pruned on what is known as the spur system as shown

Fig. 56.—VINE SPUR-PRUNED.

by fig. 56. There is nothing arbitrary as to the hight these canes should be. It is a matter of convenience or taste whether they be trained to 3 feet or 15 feet. Vines thus treated may be allowed to produce a few bunches the third year, and by the sixth year, may be fruited to the hight of 10 or 12 feet of cane if desired. Not more than two bunches of fruit should be allowed to each shoot. We give this manner of training as one of the simplest, although the system of training has but little to do with the crop.

The distance apart at which grape-vines may be planted, except the Delaware and a few of the weaker growing sorts, is about eight feet; the Delaware may be set one-third closer. Although grape-vines are hardy in nearly all sections, yet in any locality where the ther-

mometer falls to zero, it is beneficial to lay them down
close to the ground and cover them up with rough litter
before the approach of severe weather in winter, allowing
it to remain on in spring until the buds begin to swell,
when the vines are uncovered and tied up to the trellis.
If covered in this way they should be pruned before laying down. Pruning may be done at any time from November to March. It is a common belief that grape-vines
should be pruned only at certain seasons. The weather
must not be too cold, otherwise it is supposed they may
be injured if then pruned. Again, they must not be
pruned late in the spring, else the sap oozing from the
cuts may bleed them to death. Let me say that both
these notions are utter nonsense. The pruning of any
tree or vine in the coldest weather cannot possibly injure,
and the "bleeding" or running of the sap after any ordinary pruning, can no more hurt the vine than the
blood flowing from a pin scratch would weaken a healthy
man. This method of covering up the grape-vine is not
commonly practised, but we are satisfied that in exposed
positions it is well worth the trouble. I have practised
it with vines now ten years old, embracing some 20 varieties ; my soil is a stiff clay very unsuitable for the grape,
yet these vines have kept clear of mildew, when my
neighbor's vines a few hundred yards off have been seriously injured by it. I have long believed that intense
cold, long continued, is hurtful to even such plants as we
call hardy, and the wonderful vigor of these old vines,
so treated, seems a good evidence of it.

The litter used in covering, (which has become well-
rotted by spring), is spread over the border, acting both
as a summer mulch and fertilizer. Mildew is the worst
enemy to the vine ; the same remedy we recommend in
this book for mildew on roses, will be found equally effi-
cacious for the grape. On the large scale dry sulphur is
used, blown upon the vines by a bellows for the purpose.

Propagation of the grape is done by nurserymen in green-houses, similar to that used for propagating florists plants. But most of the varieties can be grown with fair success by cuttings in the open air. The cuttings, (made from the young, well ripened shoots of the previous year's growth), may be made with two (fig. 57) or three buds or eyes, planted in rows, say one foot apart and three inches between the cuttings, and set so that the top eye or bud only is above ground. The situation where the cuttings are placed should be well exposed to the sun, the soil rich and deep, and of sandy or light character. Care must be taken that the cutting is well firmed in the soil. The cuttings may be made from the prunings at any time during winter, and kept in a damp cellar or buried outside in sand until planted in the cutting-bed in the spring.

Fig. 57.
CUTTING.

THE VARIETIES OF THE GRAPE

Now number many hundred, and we will recommend only a very few of the most distinct sorts that have been grown long enough to allow us to be certain of their merits.

Concord is perhaps more universally cultivated than any other. It grows most luxuriantly, bearing bunches of large size abundantly ; color black, with a rich blue bloom ; the flavor is of average quality. Ripens during the month of September.

Hartford Prolific.—Resembles the Concord in general appearance, but ripens two or three weeks earlier. It is valuable on this account, but in light soils drops its fruit badly, which is quite a drawback.

Iona.—Is a seedling of the old Catawba, color pale red,

flavor excellent, fully equal to the Catawba, but it is preferable to that variety in ripening fully a month earlier, or from the 1st to 15th of September. One of the best, where it succeeds; it requires a strong soil.

Delaware.—Its entirely distinct character from any of our hardy grapes, at one time raised the question whether this was not a foreign variety, but that point we believe is now settled, and it is conceded to be a native. In flavor it is unsurpassed, equal to many of our best foreign sorts. Bunches and berries small, of a dark pinkish red color.

Rogers' Hybrids.—These varieties, probably from the unfortunate mistake made by their raiser in designating them by numbers instead of by names, have never, we think, had the popularity they deserve. Some of them are entirely distinct in color and flavor from any other native grapes, and form magnificent bunches. No. 4 (now called Wilder), has berries and bunches of the largest size, black with rich bloom, flavor excellent, ripens September first. No. 15, (Agawam), is a beautiful grape of a bronze color, with pinkish bloom on the side next the sun. It ripens early in September, and we find every season that the grape consumers of our household rarely touch a bunch of any other grape as long as any are left on No. 15. No. 1, (Gœthe), is about the size and color of the white Malaga grape of commerce, tinged with pink on the sunny side, flavor excellent, one of the latest, ripening here in October. No. 19 resembles No. 4, but of an entirely distinct flavor, by some preferred; ripens 15th of September.

CHAPTER XLVI.

THE COLD GRAPERY.

I know of no addition to a country home from which such a large amount of satisfaction can be obtained at so small an outlay as from a grapery for growing the different varieties of foreign grapes. It has been proved that none of these fine varieties can be cultivated with any satisfaction in any part of the northern or even middle states, except under glass. In California and some other states and territories west of the Mississippi the varieties of the European grape have been extensively grown in the open air. There the conditions of climate are such as to make their culture a success equal to that attained any where in Europe. Besides the luxury of the grape as a table fruit, no finer sight can be seen, and there is nothing of which an amateur gardener may be more proud than a grapery in which the vines are loaded with ripe fruit. And as this can be obtained at a trifling original outlay, and with but little attention in the cultivation afterwards, I will briefly describe how to do it.

Our climate is particularly well adapted to the cultivation of vines under glass without fire heat, and the wonder is that cold graperies are not in more general use even by people of moderate means than they at present are. We built one for our own use on the plan shown on page 92; it answering for a greenhouse as well as for a grapery. The dimensions are 50 feet long by 25 wide. It is finished in very good style, and cost but little more than $1,000. It was planted in June, and the third year from planting we cut upwards of 300 lbs. of fruit from it ; the next season it yielded nearly double that quantity. The building was begun by setting locust posts four feet apart ; on these was framed the sill, on the front of which were placed upright sashes two and a half feet in hight, and on these the gutter. From the gutter was sprung the bars, ten inches apart each way, running on the east side clear to the ridge pole ; on the west framed to within 2 feet of it, so as to give room for lifting sashes. These were two feet wide by six long. To these sashes, eight in number, were attached Hitching's patent ventilating apparatus, which by turning a crank opens these sashes from one to twenty-four inches, as desired. The front sashes may be made so that every alternate one can open outward. The glass used is known as second quality English or French, 8 x 10 inches, and put in without the use of any putty on the top of the glass, the manner of glazing being to "bed" the pane in soft putty, pressing it down tightly, and then tacking in the glass with large glazing points about the size shown in fig. 58; we find it an excellent plan in glazing to turn up the edge of these points as in fig. 59, so that they can catch under the edge of the lapping pane to keep it in

Fig. 58.
TIN.

Fig. 59.
BENT TIN.

place, otherwise it would slip down, and give a great deal of trouble. Glaziers will not use the points in this way unless compelled to do so, as it takes a somewhat longer time. Glass should never be lapped more than a quarter of an inch, if much more, the water gets between the laps, and when it freezes the glass is cracked. With these instructions about the erection of the glass and wood-work, any intelligent mechanic should be able to build from the plan given. Provision for water should be made by building a cistern inside the grapery, say four feet deep by eight feet in diameter, or that capacity in an oblong shape would be better. This cistern can be supplied by water from the roof, having a waste-pipe for overflow. These general directions for such a structure

7

as shown in the cut, are equally applicable for almost any size or kind of grapery. Many are built in the form of a "lean-to," that is, placed against any building or fence, using such for the back wall of the grapery. This would necessitate only the low front wall, which need not be more than one foot from the ground, if the width is but ten or twelve feet, but a path would require to be sunk inside to give room to stand upright. The sketch, fig.

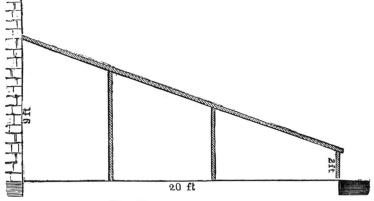

Fig. 60.—LEAN-TO GRAPERY.

60, shows an outline of a " lean-to " grapery twenty feet wide, nine feet high at back and two feet in front. Such a structure, (exclusive of the " border,") may be put up roughly at a cost not exceeding $4 per running foot, without heating apparatus. Its aspect may be any point from east to south-west.

I recollect that some dozen years ago a German jeweler in Jersey City, N. J., grew a splendid crop of Black Hamburgs on vines which had been planted against the rear fence of his city lot, by placing against the fence some old sashes eight feet long. It was rather a bungling sort of an arrangement and awkward to get at, but it served the purpose of ripening the Hamburg grapes, which could not have been done without the glass. When one contemplates the erection of a complete range of graperies, the services of a competent garden architect should be engaged. The border of the one we have in use was begun by excavating the natural soil to the depth of twenty inches and fifteen feet in width, for the length of the grapery on each side. The inside was left untouched, the borders being entirely outside. The bottom of the excavation was graded from the front of the building to the outside of the borders, with a fall of about an inch to a foot, so that thorough and rapid drainage would be sure to be attained. At the extremity of each border a drain was built to carry off the water. The whole bottom was then cemented over so as to prevent the roots from penetrating the subsoil. This pit was then filled to the depth of about two feet, (four inches being allowed for settling), with a compost which was previously prepared by mixing about three parts of turf taken from the surface of a rather shaly pasture, one part of rotten stable manure, and one part of lime rubbish.

It is one of the popular errors that vines for graperies should be two or three years old; the age of a vine usually has but little to do with its size, and if grape-vines are properly grown the first year from cuttings, they will be quite as good for planting as if two or three years old. In fact it is a question whether a vine grown from a cutting in March, and planted in June, is not quite as good as one a year older. Our experience has shown that there is hardly a perceptible difference in the two at the end of the season ; as such vines, however, are too tender to be shipped far, we generally recommend buying one year old vines that may be planted in April, May, or June, having ripened shoots about three feet in length. These vines are all grown in pots the previous season, and when received the soil should be shaken off entirely, and the roots spread out in the border without injuring them. The root, it will be understood, is planted *outside* in the border, and the shoot taken inside, through an opening in the walls. This is made of brick or stone, and should be left open at every three feet, the distance at which the vines should be planted ; if the wall is of wood, it can easily be cut to suit the size of the vine. The plants we used were strong one-year-old vines, and were set about June 1st. By October they had grown to over twenty feet in length. The varieties used were nine-tenths Black Hamburg, with a few Muscats and Frontignans, all of which have done exceedingly well.

In November they were cut back to the bottom of the rafter, or about three feet from the ground, and quickly reached the top again the second year, with firm, well-ripened wood. In November they were again pruned back to about three feet above the foot of the rafter, or six feet from the ground. On this shoot was produced the fruit referred to, (the third year from the time of planting). We prune any time in November or December after the leaves have fallen, and cut the shoot back to about four feet from top of the rafter, or about sixteen feet from the ground.

Every December we lay the vines down along the front wall after being pruned, covering them completely with soil until May, when they are then taken up and tied to the wires, which are $1|_{16}$ galvanized iron, and run across the rafters 15 inches apart and 15 inches from the glass. The training followed is what is called the "spur" system, which is simply to allow one cane or shoot to each rafter, (or at three feet apart), and pruning the side shoots or "bearing wood" annually back to one eye. In the summer treatment of the cold grapery, the principle must never be lost sight of, that to keep the vines in perfect health, a temperature of not less than 70° at night, with 10° or 15° higher during the day is always necessary. Any rapid variation downward is certain to result in mildew. The floor of the grapery should be kept dashed with water at all times, unless in damp weather, from the time the buds start in May, until the fruit begins to ripen in September, except during the period the vines are in flower, when it should be dispensed with until the fruit is set. If the weather is dry, copious watering is necessary for the border outside. The summer pruning of the grapery consists simply in pinching off the laterals, or side shoots which start from where the leaf joins the stem, to one leaf. Every winter three inches of the best well-rotted stable manure is spread over the border, and over that six inches of leaves or litter ; this is raked off in spring, and the manure forked in, the object being to feed the roots from the top of the border. This same treatment we give our hardy grapes with excellent results.

I am a good deal of a utilitarian, and am very apt to make even my luxuries "pay" when it is practicable to do so ; and though we would hardly think of selling our grapes that have been grown for private use, yet I do not scruple to make the glass that shelters them do double duty by using it in winter to shelter our half-hardy roses from November to May. Those that do not make rose-growing a business, as I do, can nevertheless profit by my example, and use the cold grapery for many purposes during the winter months when it is not needed for the grape-vines. Besides roses, all plants of a half-hardy character may be kept there, such as Pomegranates, Crape Myrtles, Pampas Grass, Tritomas, Carnations, etc., care being taken that the pots or tubs in which they are planted are plunged in leaves, tan, or some such substance, so the roots do not freeze. The cold grapery makes an excellent poultry-house in winter, only if put to that use, care must be taken that the buried vines are secure against the scratching of the hens.

CHAPTER XLVII.

THE HOT-HOUSE OR FORCING GRAPERY.

When grapes are forced by artificial heat, probably the best plan is that of the "lean-to" structure shown by the illustrations, figs. 61, 62, and 63. Fig. 61 gives the plan, which, as in some former engravings, it is not practicable to show on the page at full length; it is accordingly "fractured" portions, as shown by the irregular lines, being taken out of each compartment; the figures give the proper proportion. Fig. 62 is a part of the front elevation, and fig. 63, a section at the division between the two houses. The house is 100 feet long by 16 feet wide, divided into two compartments for early and late forcing, each 50 x 16 feet, and both heated by one boiler with valves in the furnace pit to shut off and taps to draw the water from the pipes not in use ; a matter to be looked to when vineries are not in use, for if the water is not drawn out of the pipes it may freeze and burst them. When grapes are to be forced, it is essential that a sufficient covering of manure or leaves be placed on the border to prevent frost from reaching the roots, as to apply heat to the vines inside while the roots are frozen, would seriously injure them. For very early forcing, when the vines are started as early as January, it is usual not only to put covering enough to secure from frost, but also to slightly ferment, so as to throw some warmth into the border. No matter at what season the grapery is started for forcing, the temperature should not run over 50° or 55° at night, with a day temperature of 10° or 15° higher, increasing 10° when the buds have opened, which will be in four or five weeks from the time of starting. In five or six weeks the fruit will be set and the temperature is to be raised 10° more. In forcing, moisture is of equal im-

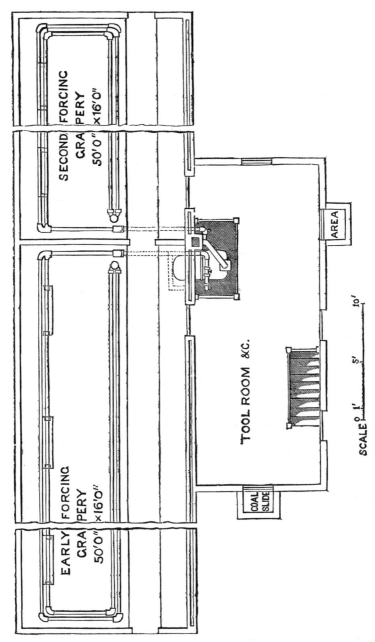

Fig. 61.—PLAN OF FORCING GRAPERY.

portance with heat, for if this is not attended to, you may expect red-spiders and thrips, and then all your labor may be in vain ; to keep up this moisture, tanks are usu-

Fig. 62.—ELEVATION OF FRONT OF FORCING GRAPERY (IN PART).

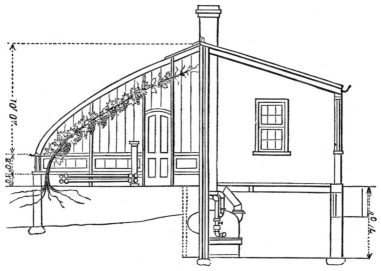

Fig. 63.—SECTION OF FORCING GRAPERY.

ally placed on the hot-water pipes for graperies, and these are kept filled with water, keeping up a continued evaporation, except at the time the vines are in flower; it should be then discontinued until the fruit is set. When there is no such arrangement for evaporation, dash water over the floors and use the syringe. To secure fine berries and bunches, one-third of the berries should be thinned out when of the size of peas, using scissors made for this purpose.

CHAPTER XLVIII.

THE STRAWBERRY.

Of all small fruits, none perhaps stand so high in general favor as the strawberry. Its culture is simple, and as it grows freely in almost any soil or location, no garden of any pretensions should be without it. If a choice of soil can be had, nothing is so suitable as a deep, rich, but rather sandy loam, though it will yield returns sufficient to warrant its cultivation on any soil, from almost pure sand to clay, providing that it is drained naturally or artificially. In all soils, deep spading or plowing is essential to the production of fine crops ; and this should not be less than a foot, and if 18 inches, all the better. A coat of thoroughly rotted stable manure at least three inches in thickness, should be dug in and well mixed with the soil to a depth of six or nine inches. In the absence of stable manure, any of the concentrated fertilizers mentioned in chapter VI, "How to Use Concentrated Fertilizers," used in the manner and quantities there described, will do as a substitute. Where muck from the swamps, or leaf-mold from the woods can be obtained, twenty bushels of either of these mixed with one bushel of ashes, will make an excellent fertilizer for strawberries, and may be spread on as thickly as stable manure, and on sandy soils is probably better.

Strawberries may be planted either in the fall or spring. If the plants are to be set in the fall, it should not be done if possible in this latitude before the middle of September.   This, of course, refers to the plants from runners taken up from the bed in the usual manner, and there is nothing gained in time over planting the next spring, as the plant must grow for one season before it can bear a full crop of fruit.   In private gardens it is

Fig. 64.—STRIKING STRAWBERRIES IN POTS.

much better to have the plants layered in pots, as they may then be set at almost any time.   These pots may be from two to three inches in diameter ; when a lot of strawberry plants are wanted for a new bed, all that is necessary to do is to fill these small pots with soil, and "plunge" or plant the pot just to the surface level, placing the unrooted "runner" of the strawberry plant on the top of the soil in the flower-pot, and laying a small stone or clod on it to keep it in place.   This method of striking in pots is shown in fig. 64.   The runners so treated will form plants in two or three weeks, and may be planted out with safety any time from August to October. If strawberry plants are treated in this way, and planted in August, and care taken that all runners that come from them be cut off as soon as formed, so that the whole force of the root is thrown into the main crown, a full crop of berries will be gathered the season following, or in nine or ten months from time of planting. We have practiced this system of layering strawberry plants in pots for what we need for our own use, for the past twenty years, and the results have been so successful that we have many converts to the system among our neighbors. Plants grown in this manner cannot often be obtained from the nurseries, as the necessary labor and expense of the pots makes the price five times more than that of ordinary plants rooted in the open bed. When strawberry plants are set out in the fall, unless under favorable circumstances, many will fail to grow, for the reason that each young plant or runner is sustained in part by the old plant, and when detached, feels the shock more than a rooted cutting or seedling plant does, that has been growing for weeks on its own account, for that reason we have always advised all that were intending to plant fresh strawberry beds, to prepare their plants a few weeks ahead by layering them in pots. Two to four hundred plants are all that an ordinary family will need, and two or three hours' work would be all the time required to layer the plants in the pots. One hundred plants so prepared, will give more fruit the first season than 1,000 plants planted in the usual way, and the plant forms a stool quicker, and much less time is expended in keeping them clean. The use of layered plants is recommended specially for fall planting, and the sooner it is done in fall the better; plant in August if possible.

In spring the use of potted plants would have no special advantage, as if planted in April or May, they would

have all the summer to grow, but of course no fruit can
be expected the season of planting.   For this reason, it
will be seen that to secure a crop quickly, the time to
plant is in August or September, and from plants that
have been layered in pots.   There is no arbitrary rule for
the distance apart at which strawberry plants should be
set, but if the ground has been prepared as advised,
the finest fruit will be had by giving them plenty of
room.   For our own use we usually set 400 plants annually in August, at two feet apart between the rows, and
eighteen inches between the plants, and gather about 200
quarts of splendid fruit.   If the ground is limited they
may be planted at half the above distance, particularly if
set late in fall.   There is one very important point in
strawberry culture that should never be neglected; that
is, that the beds be entirely covered with hay, straw, or
leaves, to the depth of three or four inches.   This covering should not be put on, however, before the approach
of severe weather, in this district about the middle of December.   This covering should not be taken off in spring;
it is only necessary to go over the beds as soon as growth
begins in spring, and pull the covering back from the
plants only sufficient to expose the crown, allowing all to
remain on the bed.   This covering serves several purposes.   It keeps the roots warm until the plants start to
grow, it keeps the fruit clean when ripe, it prevents the
growth of weeds, and finally acts as a mulch to keep the
soil from drying in hot weather.   Although strawberry
beds will remain in bearing for a number of years, the
fruit is always largest and finest the first season of bearing, gradually getting smaller as the plants get older.
hence it is desirable to provide for a succession, if not
every year, at least every second year.   For garden culture in this, as in all other fruits, it is unwise to use any
but fully tested varieties, three or four of which are
sufficient.

VARIETIES OF THE STRAWBERRY.

Triomphe de Gand is one of the favorite varieties; it is of large size, fine flavor, and a fair bearer. It requires a heavy soil.

Wilson's Seedling is a variety better known than any other sort; it bears large crops, but is very sour. It is much used for preserving.

Champion.—A berry of an immense size, and beautiful dark crimson appearance, an abundant bearer, but not so rich in flavor as some others.

Charles Downing.—This variety is likely to take the place of the Wilson, as it has all the productiveness of that; succeeds on all soils, and a much better berry.

Kentucky.—Is the latest variety, and by planting it with earlier sorts, will extend the season several days.

Black Defiance.—This is a first-class fruit in every respect, large, productive, and of high flavor; while its dark color unfits it for market, it is one of the best for the private garden.

Seth Boyden.—One of the largest berries, very productive, sweet, but not very high flavored; its long neck allows it to be hulled very readily.

FORCING STRAWBERRIES.

Those who have a greenhouse often wish to force strawberries into fruit several weeks in advance of the time that they will be ripe in the open air. It may be done in a frame or pit. The young runners must be first layered in pots, as already described, as early as runners are formed, and as soon as the small pots are filled with roots, they must be shifted into larger ones, say six inches in diameter, the runners being pinched off as they appear, so as to throw the whole strength of the plant into the fruiting crown. The soil in which to pot strawberries for

forcing is the one we recommend for nearly all plants;
three parts rotted sods, and one part rotted manure.
The potted strawberries should be placed on boards,
flagging, or a layer of coal ashes, to prevent the earth-
worms from getting in at the bottom of the pots. At
first, after being shifted, they should be set closely together, but as they grow they must be spread apart, as it
is necessary that the air pass around the pots to ripen the
roots. Of course the necessary attention to water is as
important with these as with other plants in pots. They
may thus stand in the open air until November, when
the pots may be plunged in dry leaves to prevent their being broken by frost; and the tops also covered an inch or
two with the same material; as cold weather advances,
they may be taken in at intervals of two weeks or so and
placed on the shelves of a greenhouse, near the glass,
where the temperature will average at night 50 degrees,
and if due attention to watering has been given, a crop
will be the result, such as will well repay the labor,
not only as fruit, but the plants so loaded will themselves be beautiful greenhouse ornaments. Good varieties for forcing are Triomphe de Gand and Champion.

RASPBERRY.

To have the Raspberry in perfection, the same preparation of soil is necessary as for the Strawberry. The canes
or shoots of the Raspberry are biennial; that is, the cane
or shoot that is formed one season, bears fruit the next
season, and dies off after fruiting, giving place to the
young cane that is to fruit the following season, and
so on. The distances apart to plant the Raspberry for
garden culture, may be, if in rows, five feet apart, with
the plants two feet apart in the row, or if in separate
stools or hills, they may be set four feet each way. If
planted at distances of four feet apart, three plants may
be put in each "hill," which will quicker secure a crop.

They may be set either in fall or in spring ; if in fall, a covering of four or five inches of litter should be spread over the roots to prevent them from getting too much frozen. And even when the plants are established and growing, it is necessary in many cold sections, to bend down the canes and cover them with pine branches or some covering that will shield them from severe freezing. On the large scale the canes are bent down and covered with a few inches of earth, an operation that may be rapidly performed by two persons. One bends down the

Fig. 65.—LAYING DOWN RASPBERRY CANES.

canes, (using a pitchfork or other implement), as shown in the accompanying diagram, (fig. 65), while the other throws sufficient earth near the tips to hold the canes in place ; after a row is thus bent over, the two go back and cover with earth more completely. All the pruning that is necessary for the Raspberry is to thin out the shoots in each hill to four or six ; this is best done in the summer after the fruit is gathered, and at the same time the old canes that have borne the fruit should be cut out, so that the young shoots, coming forward to do duty next season, may have room to grow freely, and develop and ripen the wood. When the leaves drop in fall, the canes may be shortened down a foot or so, which will complete the pruning process. To get the full benefit of all the fruit, it is very necessary to stake the Raspberry, this may be done either by tying the canes of each plant separately to a stout stake, driven two feet or so in the ground, or if grown in rows they may be tied to wires running along the rows ; the wires should be stretched between two stout posts, one at each end of the row, and three feet more or less above the ground, according to variety ; to prevent the wire from sagging, stakes should be driven into the ground directly under it, at intervals of six or ten feet ; the wire is attached to these by means of staples placed over it and driven into the ends of the stakes. The diagram, fig. 66, shows the method of training to the wire ; the longer canes at the right and left are the canes which are to fruit the current year ; these are tied out as there shown, while the new shoots, which

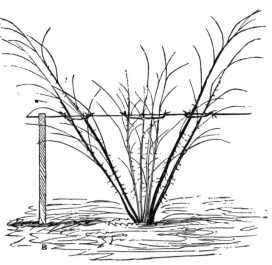

Fig. 66.—TRAINING RASPBERRIES TO A WIRE.

are to furnish canes for the next year's fruiting, grow up in the center, and as soon as tall enough are tied to the wire ; after the outer canes have fruited, they are cut away to give the others more room.

The varieties are very numerous, those named below are such as will be most satisfactory for private use. From 100 to 200 hills or plants, of all varieties, will usually be sufficient for most families.

Fastolff.—A large crimson fruit of delicious flavor.

Brinckle's Orange.—An orange colored berry of large size, very productive, and of excellent flavor.

Clarke.—Not quite so large as the Fastolff, but of

strong, robust habit, enduring well the extremes of heat and cold.

Philadelphia.—One of the hardiest and most productive, growing in soils and situations where the others would fail. It is of rather poor quality, but is useful for the above reasons.

Catawissa.—A fall-bearing variety of medium size, color purplish crimson, medium flavor.

BLACK CAPS.

Black-caps or Black Raspberries have become very popular of late years, many persons being fond of their peculiar flavor. They belong to a distinct species from the ordinary Raspberries ; the plants make no suckers, but propagate themselves by taking root at the ends of the long branches, which in the fall, if allowed to grow at will, bend over and reach the earth. They throw up shoots from the base of the plant which take the place of those which have already borne a crop. In gardens where there is no desire to propagate the plants, the growing shoots should be pinched off when they get three or four feet high, and any side-shoots they may throw off are stopped by pinching when they are about 18 inches long. The bearing wood is thinned out after the fruit is off.

Mammoth Cluster is considered the most productive of all the numerous varieties.

Thornless.—This is preferable to the others in being nearly free from spines, and though the fruit is not quite so large, it is much more easily gathered.

BLACKBERRY.

The cultivation of the Blackberry is nearly similar to that of the Raspberry, except that it should be planted about one-third farther apart, and it being hardier, there is no need for covering it in winter. As it has a more

vigorous growth, it is sometimes set in any out of the
way corner, and in almost any soil ; but it will amply
repay generous cultivation with finer fruit.   The manner of growth is the same as the Raspberry, and when
the fruit is picked, the old canes are to be cut out to give
the new ones a chance. The new shoots are very vigorous
growers, and when they reach the hight of five, or at
most, six feet, they should be stopped by pinching ; this
will cause an abundance of side shoots to start which are
to be pinched when about 18 inches long.   This treatment increases the productiveness of the plants and keeps
the fruit within reach.   The bushes should be kept tied
to stout stakes or wires, as advised for the Raspberry.

The following are a few of the popular kinds :

Kittatinny.—An immensely large berry of excellent
flavor, of deep, shiny black color, one of the very best
for family use.

Wilson's Early.—One of the earliest varieties, ripening a week or more before the Kittatinny, quite as large,
and of excellent quality.

Cut-leaved.—The merit of this variety is its lateness of
ripening, coming in just when the others are done fruiting.   It is of large size, and esteemed by many, while
others do not like its very distinct and peculiar flavor.

CURRANTS.

The Currant is useful both for dessert and for preserving purposes.   An immense weight of fruit is obtained
for the space it occupies, and the ease of its culture makes
it common in every garden.   The red and white varieties
of Currants may be planted three or four feet apart each
way, the black at four or five feet apart.   Pruning is
done in fall by cutting off about one-third of the young
growth of the previous summer, and thinning out old
shoots when the plant gets too thick.   All are trained in

low bush form, the whites and reds usually from three to four feet high and wide, and the black four to six feet. An insect known as the currant-worm is often very destructive. On its first appearance, if confined to a few leaves, these should be cut off, shoot and all, and destroyed. If they threaten to be troublesome, powdered white Hellebore, either dusted on, or mixed four ounces to a pailful of water and applied with a syringe, will destroy them at once.

Black Naples.—This is the favorite black variety, and is used almost exclusively for jams and jellies. The black varieties are much less grown here than in Europe, but the taste for them is increasing.

Red Dutch.—Color of berries deep red, of average size, flavor excellent.

White Grape.—Berries large, of a yellowish-white color. The flavor of this variety is less acid than any other ; excellent for dessert.

Versailles.—The fruit much larger than the Red Dutch, and the best flavored of all the large-berried kinds.

Cherry.—Berries larger than that of any other sort, but too acid for most tastes ; only suitable for jelly.

GOOSEBERRY.

The Gooseberry is a fruit better suited for the climate of Britain than for ours, and it is never seen here in the perfection it attains there. It ripens just when our hottest weather occurs, forcing it unnaturally to maturity, and hence the absence of the size and flavor it attains when ripened at a lower temperature. The native varieties, though far inferior in quality, are usually more free from mildew, and are therefore most desirable for cultivation here, as the fruit with us is more used in the green than in the ripe state. Gooseberries are planted from three to four feet apart, and are treated in all other respects like Currant bushes.

Downing.—A native variety of medium size, greenish-white when ripe, excellent quality.

Houghton's Seedling.—Also a native variety, size medium, color red, flavor average.

Of the foreign varieties among *Reds* may be named as leading sorts, Warrington, Champion, Waterloo; of *Greens,* Green Globe, Melville, Green Gage; of *Yellows,* Sulphur, Champagne, Golden Drop; of, *Whites,* Crystal, Whitesmith, Dutch.

FIGS.

The Fig on account of it not being hardy in the northern states, is but little cultivated unless in tubs, which are placed in cellars or sheds to protect them during the winter months, or occasionally on the back wall of lean-to graperies ; but in all parts of the country where the thermometer does not get lower than twenty degrees above zero, they can be grown freely in the open air without protection. It is hardly ever necessary to prune the Fig, except to regulate its shape by cutting back any extra strong shoots. In sections of the country such as Maryland, or West Virginia, or Delaware, where it may require slight protection when grown in the open air, it should be planted against a wall or fence, and trained against it ; on the approach of cold weather it should be laid down and covered as recommended for hardy grapes. When grown in tubs to be kept in cellars, sheds, or greenhouse pits, they should be placed under cover in this latitude early in November, kept as dry as possible without shrivelling, and set out in the open air again in May. The soil and general treatment for plants grown in the open air in pots or tubs will be suitable for them.

There are numerous sorts in cultivation from which we select the following :

White Genoa.—Large roundish, yellow skin ; flesh reddish-pink, excellent flavor.

Brown Turkey.—Pear shaped, average size, brown skin ; flesh red, rich flavor.

Early Violet.—Skin brownish-red ; flesh reddish-crimson, delicious flavor; fruit rather small; one of the hardiest.

Brown Ischia.—Size large, skin yellowish-brown ; flesh violet, sweet and luscious, very prolific.

QUINCE.

A few Quince trees should be planted in every garden where there is any pretension to a collection of fruits. It is a tree requiring but little attention, and for that reason is often neglected, and very unsightly specimens are seen. The tree is very ornamental in flower and fruit, and by a little attention to pruning, a handsome head may be formed, though equally luxuriant crops are seen on trees that have been untouched for years. They may be planted eight or ten feet apart. In varieties the kind in most general use is the

Apple-shaped or Orange.—A large round variety, bright golden-yellow.

Pear-shaped is larger, color greenish-yellow, and its shape being more pear-like, readily distinguishes it from the other and better variety.

Rea's Seedling.—A variety not very abundant as yet, is the largest and finest of all.

CHERRY.

The Cherry-tree begins to bear usually in two or three years after planting trees of the size sold at the nurseries, and continues to annually enlarge in growth and productiveness until it often attains a larger size than most of our fruit-trees.   The Cherry grows freely in almost any soil that is free from moisture, preferring, however, like most other fruits, a deep loamy soil.   The tree may be trained as desired, either in pyramidal form or with a round top, by pruning and directing the shoots.   The distance apart may be ten or twelve feet.   Varieties :

Black Tartarian.—Deep purplish-black, very large ; fine flesh, unsurpassed in quality ; last of June.

Rockport.—Very large, amber-yellow, dotted red ; flesh firm, sweet and excellent ; ripens in June.

Coe's Transparent.—Color pale-amber-yellow ; spotted with pink ; flesh tender, sweet, and of fine flavor ; ripens middle of June.

May Duke.—Color dark-red, size medium, quality excellent ; ripens early in June.

Morello.—A sub-acid variety of medium size, color bright-red, changing to darker color when fully ripe ; hangs long on the tree, mainly used for pies and preserving.

PLUM.

The cultivation of the Plum is rendered nearly useless in most places by the attacks of the Curculio, or Plum Weevil.   Every conceivable application to the trees has been tried without any satisfactory result.   The only thing which will effectually save a crop in the districts infested by this insect, is to jar the tree in the morning or in cool days, first spreading sheets under the trees to catch the weevils, after which they may be burned.   If this is begun as soon as the plums are formed, and persisted in every few days until they are ripe, a large share of the crop may be saved.   This may be thought to be paying rather dear for a crop of plums, but it is really the

only way it can be secured. Many years ago the crop of
a plum orchard under our charge numbering over a hundred large trees, was saved by this process, while all other
plums in the district where the jarring of the trees was
not resorted to, were completely destroyed. This plan
was recommended nearly half a century ago, and no
other practicable method has since been presented.
It has been recommended by some to plant the trees on
the bank of a pond or running stream, and train them to
overhang the water, also to pave or cement around the
roots so that the insect cannot burrow, but these plans
would be often impossible, and are useless. Trees upon
stiff, clayey soils are more exempt from the ravages of the
Curculio than those upon light ones, probably for the
reason that the insect in the grub or larvæ state cannot
penetrate them so readily, as they must enter the ground
to become perfect insects. The average distance at which
the Plum may be planted is from ten to twelve feet. The
following are distinct and fine sorts.

Orleans.—Color purple, with a rich blue bloom, size
medium ; flesh deep yellow, flavor of first quality ; clingstone ; ripens in August.

Washington.—Color yellow, marbled with red next the
sun ; large size ; flesh firm, sweet, and rich ; freestone ;
ripens first of September.

Green Gage.—A well known variety, rather small in
size, but of exquisite flavor, color greenish-yellow, spotted
with red on the sunny side ; freestone ; ripens early in
August.

Columbia.—Of the largest size, color brownish-purple ;
flesh yellow, sweet, and finely flavored ; freestone ; ripens
the last of August.

Golden Drop.—A very old and well known sort, color
golden-yellow with red spots next the sun ; large, oval ;

rich and sweet yellowish flesh ; clingstone ; ripens middle of September.

PEACH.

The Peach prefers the light, dry, and warm soils, known as sandy loams.   The tree is shortlived in most sections, and attains its best fruiting condition usually when from five to nine years old.   The tree is greatly benefitted by pruning ; the growth of the previous season should be shortened about one-third ; this, if annually followed from the time the trees are set, will give them compact heads instead of open, straggling ones, the branches of which will break down with the first full crop of fruit.   In the peach-growing districts the cultivators do not expect more than three crops in five years, and if they get two full crops in that time they are content, and amateurs should expect no more.   When a crop sets at all there is usually more fruit than the tree can carry and ripen ; no fruit needs severe thinning more than the peach.   In bearing seasons half or two-thirds of those which set may be removed with benefit to the rest. When a tree appears sickly with yellow foliage, dig it up at once.   The distance apart may be from eight to ten feet.   Among the favorite varieties for garden culture may be named

Early Beatrice.—One of Mr. Rivers' seedlings, and so far as tried in this country promises to be a valuable early sort ; its size is small, but quality good ; freestone.

Hale's Early.—A very early peach, of fair size and great beauty, but has the fault that it in some localities rots just as it begins to ripen, a difficulty probably due to overbearing rather than to locality ; freestone, excellent.

Columbia.—Large, round, color yellow and red, streaked with dark-crimson ; flesh yellow, rich, and juicy, flavor excellent ; freestone ; ripens in September.

Crawford's Early.—Large, roundish, color yellow, tinged with red ; flesh yellow, rich, and sweet ; ripens last of August ; freestone.

Crawford's Late.—Similar in appearance, but ripening three weeks later.

Cooledge's Favorite.—Size medium, roundish oval, color clear white with crimson cheek ; flesh rich, juicy, and of first quality ; ripens in August; freestone.

Honest John, or *Early York.*—Large, roundish, white with red cheek ; flesh white, very juicy, excellent flavor; middle of August; freestone.

Morris White.—A well known variety, size medium, color greenish-white, flavor average. The variety mostly used for preserving ; middle of September ; freestone.

Malacatune.—Fruit large, yellow, with dark red cheek ; flesh orange-yellow, flavor excellent ; middle of September ; freestone.

NECTARINES.

Nectarines are only smooth skinned peaches, requiring in all respects similar treatment to the peach. They are but little grown in this country, as they are equally liable to injury by the attacks of the Plum Curculio, with the Plum itself. The same treatment recommended for its destruction in Plums, must be applied to the Nectarine. There is a peculiarity in the flavor of some varieties of Nectarines differing from that of any of the peaches, and by some they are greatly preferred to any peach in flavor. The successful varieties are not numerous.

Early Newington.—Large, roundish oval, greenish-yellow mottled red ; flesh yellowish-white ; September ; cling.

Hunt's Tawny.—Large, round, amber-yellow with red cheek ; flesh orange, melting, flavor excellent ; ripens in August ; freestone.

8

Boston.—Large, oval, yellow with mottled crimson cheek ; flesh yellow, excellent quality ; September ; free-stone.

APRICOT.

The Apricot is closely related to the peach, but belongs to another species ; it is less juicy, and has a flavor quite distinct from, and by some preferred to, that of the peach. The blighting Curculio attacks the Apricot also, and its culture can only be successful by combating the difficulties that attend that of the plum, unless in special locations that seem few and far between. The varieties are

Moorpark.—Size large as an average peach, yellow with red cheek ; flesh orange, sweet, and of exquisite flavor ; ripens in July.

Orange.—Pale yellow with red cheek, size medium ; ripens end of July.

Turkey.—Large, deep yellow, shaded orange ; flesh pale-yellow, firm, rich, and sweet ; ripens in August.

APPLE.

The apple can only be grown in gardens as a dwarf, either kept in a bush form or trained as a pyramid or other shape. The dwarf trees are made so by grafting on dwarfing stocks, while the varieties are the same as those found in the large trees of the orchard. Two sorts of dwarfing stocks are used by nurserymen, the Doucin and Paradise. Trees upon the Doucin will ultimately grow quite large, and as the Paradise is the only stock which makes really dwarf trees, the amateur who wishes to grow dwarf apple-trees should make sure that they are worked on Paradise stocks. Of course trees of this kind are not advised as a source of fruit, but there can scarcely be a handsomer object in the garden than a bush three feet high, and about the same through, loaded with enormous apples. Dwarf apple-trees may be planted six feet apart each way, while ordinary trees in the orchard are given 15 to 30 feet, or even 40 feet. The following sorts are recommended for garden culture. For descriptions see nursery catalogues. Red Astrachan, Alexander, Sweet Bough, Fall Pippin, Gravenstein, Maiden's Blush, Porter, Rambo, Northern Spy, Mother, Twenty Ounce, Beauty of Kent, Hawthornden, Spitzenberg, Jonathan, King of Tompkins County, Keswick Codlin, Lady Apple, Red Canada, Swaar.

PEARS,

Like apples, are grown as dwarfs and standards. The former being planted from eight to ten feet apart, the latter from ten to twelve feet. The dwarfs, budded on the quince stock, are mostly used for garden culture, as from their habit they are more suitable, besides having the invaluable quality of coming quicker into bearing. Time was when the adage went, "He that plants pears, plants for his heirs," but this is now no more applicable to the pear than to the peach, for we now have fine crops of pears budded on the quince in three to five years from the time of planting. The trees may be grown as pyramids, or in the bush form, or in small gardens, pear, peach, and other trees are successfully trained in what is called the oblique cordon, which allows a number of varieties to be grown in a small space. Only a general outline of the method can be given here, referring for fuller details to Barry's and other works on fruit culture. A trellis is built about 8 feet high, by nailing a strong top and bottom rail to posts, which should be about 8 feet apart. Slats of inch stuff are put on between the two rails at an angle of 30°; these are fastened on with screws, as when the trees have reached the top, the slats are to be brought down to 45°, and they should be long enough to allow for doing

this. Young trees are set in an inclined position in a
line with these slats, which are three feet apart. Each
tree is cut back to a few buds, and one shoot allowed to
grow from the strongest bud, all the others being removed. This shoot as it grows is kept tied to the slat,
and when it throws out side-shoots, as it soon will,
they are pinched back to three or four leaves, whenever
the shoot is sufficiently developed to allow the number
of the leaves to be seen. By growing in this inclined

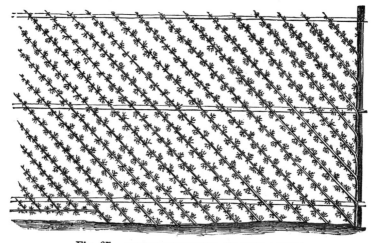

Fig. 67.—CORDON-TRAINING OF PEAR TREES.

position, and by pinching every shoot back to three or
four leaves, the tree is dwarfed and made to bear early,
and when properly managed, forms a perfect cordon or
garland, with fruit along its whole length. Fig. 67
shows a portion of a trellis of this kind. The following
varieties are recommended for either kind of training.
For descriptions see nursery catalogues. Bartlett, Beurré
d'Anjou, Duchesse d'Angoulême, Lawrence, Clapp's
Favorite, Beurré Bosc, Dana's Hovey, Vicar of Wink-
field, Howell, Urbaniste, Seckel, Winter Nelis, Brandy-
wine, Doyenné d' Eté, Louise Bonne de Jersey, Belle
Lucrative, Doyenné Boussock.

VEGETABLE GARDEN.

CHAPTER XLIX.

COTTAGE GARDENING—A DIGRESSION.

Before taking up the subject of vegetable culture, I will relate an incident connected with cottage gardening that may interest if it does not benefit some of those into whose hands this book may fall. About a dozen years ago I had the pleasure of making the acquaintance of a gentleman whose duties compelled him to be at his desk in a close office in the City of New York, from 9 o'clock A. M. to 4 P. M. Being naturally of a weak constitution, his sedentary life soon made him the victim of dyspepsia to such a degree that he felt that he must soon resign his situation. He was then a man of forty, entirely ignorant of anything pertaining to country life, and it was with great misgivings and reluctance that, by the advice of his physician, he changed his home from a closely built part of New York to a cottage in the then country-like suburb of Bergen Heights, N. J. His means enabled him to purchase a modest cottage built on a lot 50 by 150 feet ; he did not want the land, he said, but the cottage was such as he fancied, and the ground had to go with it. It was about this time that I formed his acquaintance, through some business transaction, and he asked my professional advice as to what he could do with his land, which he had already begun to consider somewhat of an incumbrance. I replied to him that, if I was not greatly mistaken, in his little plot of ground lay a cure for all his bodily ills, and that besides it could add to the comforts if not the luxuries of his table if he would only work it. "I work it !" he exclaimed. "You don't suppose that these hands could dig or delve," holding up his thin and bloodless fingers, "and if they could I know nothing about gardening." I told him I thought neither objection insurmountable if he once begun.

The result of our conversation was, that he resolved to try, and try he did to a purpose. Our interview was in March, and before the end of April he had his lot all nicely dug over, the labor being done by his own hands during an hour and a half each morning. His custom was to get up at six o'clock and work at his garden until half past seven. This gave him ample time to dress, get breakfast, and be at his desk in the city by nine. The labor of merely digging was (to him) heavy and rather monotonous, but he stuck to it bravely, and when he again presented himself before me for plants and seeds and information as to what to do with them, it was with some pride that I saw my prescription had worked so well, for my friend then looked more like a farmer than a pallid clerk. The regulating of his little garden was a simple matter, and was done according to the following diagram :

Cauliflower, cabbage and lettuce.	Strawberries.
Cucumbers, onions, and parsley.	Raspberries.
Beets, carrots, and parsnips.	Tomatoes.
Bush beans.	Asparagus and Rhubarb.

During his first season, of course, he made some blunders and some failures, but his interest in the work increased year by year. His family was supplied with an abundance of all the fresh vegetables and fruits his limited space could admit of being grown—a supply that it would have taken at least $150 to purchase at retail, and stale at that. But the benefit derived from the cultivation of this cottage garden was health—strong, rugged health—that for the six years he was my neighbor, never once failed him.

I know this case is an extremely exceptional one, for I never knew another man who so resolutely worked himself into health. There are hundreds of business men, book-keepers, salesmen, clerks, and the like who live in the suburbs of all great cities, many of whom can ill afford to pay for the keeping of the plots surrounding their cottages, but who think they can far less afford to do the work themselves. As a consequence, in nine cases out of ten, the rear, at least, of their suburban plots is a wilderness of weeds. But this is not the least of the evils, the owner has a certain amount of muscular force, and this, be it more or less, being unused, its possessor pays the penalty of his laziness in dyspepsia, and a host of other ills. The proofs are apparent everywhere that garden operations are conducive to health and longevity. The work is not unduly laborious, and when fairly entered into has a never-failing interest. The growing and the watching of the great variety of plants gives a healthy tone to the mind, while the physical labor demanded by cultivation takes care of the body.

CHAPTER L.

THE VEGETABLE GARDEN.

It is perhaps best that the space allotted to vegetables should be at one side of the garden, and that for fruits at the other, at least in the beginning, though a rotation of crops or change of position may be advantageous in course of time. I will give in brief the culture of each vegetable in general use, placing them alphabetically for easy reference, and enumerate the leading varieties.

ASPARAGUS—(*Asparagus officinalis.*)

Asparagus should be planted the first spring that the owner comes into possession of the land, and if the house is yet to be built, let the Asparagus-bed be planted at once, as it takes the roots two or three years to acquire sufficient strength to give a crop. For an ordinary family a bed of six rows of fifty or sixty feet in length, and three feet apart, will be sufficient, the plants in the rows being set nine inches apart. In planting it is customary to use two-year-old plants, but it often happens that as large a plant is raised from seed in good soils in one year as in a poorer soil in two years ; in such cases the one-year-old plant is preferable. The preparation of the Asparagus bed should be made with more care than for most vegetables, from the fact that it is a permanent crop which ought to yield as well at the end of twenty-five as of five years, if the soil has been well prepared. The asparagus bed, to start with, should be on ground thoroughly drained, either naturally or artificially, and if choice can be had, on a rather light sandy loam. This should be trenched and mixed with sufficient manure to form a coating of at least six inches thick over the bed ; this manure should be worked into the soil by trenching to the depth of two feet, as the roots of the plant will reach quite that depth in a few years. In setting, the crowns of the plants should be placed at least three inches below the surface. It makes but little difference whether it is planted in spring or fall ; if in spring, it should be done as early as the ground is dry enough to work, and if in fall, just as soon as the plants can be had, which is usually in the early part of October. We prefer fall planting on light. well-drained soils, for the reason that if it is done then, young roots are formed, which are ready to grow on the approach of spring, but if the planting is done in March or April, this formation of new roots has to take place then, and causes a corresponding delay in growth. Plants are sold by market gardeners and seedsmen, and as it will save a year or two, to purchase them, it is not worth while to raise them from seed in a private garden. The edible portion is the undeveloped stems, which if cut away as soon as they appear, are followed by others, which start from the crown of the plant. The cutting,

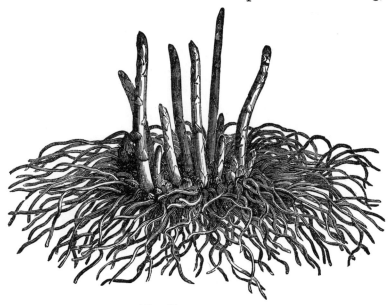

Fig. 68.—ASPARAGUS.

if continued too long, would finally exhaust the root, hence it is customary to stop cutting as soon as early peas become plenty, and allow the remaining shoots to grow during the remainder of the season, and thus accumulate sufficient strength in the plant to allow it to produce another crop of shoots the next season. The engraving, (fig. 68), represents a strong plant with the earth removed from the roots ; the shoots are shown in different stages of development, and it will be seen how readily careless cutting may injure the buds which are ready to produce a succession of shoots.

The surface of the Aspargus bed should have a top-dressing of three or four inches of rough stable manure every fall, (November), which should be lightly forked into the bed in spring. The best variety is what is known as "Van Sicklen's Colossal." In some localities Asparagus is attacked by an insect called the Asparagus Beetle. The best method of getting rid of this pest, that we have found, is to coop up a hen and let the chickens pick up the insects and their eggs.

Fig. 69.—GLOBE ARTICHOKE.

ARTICHOKE-GLOBE—
(*Cynara Scolymus.*)

The portion used of this plant is the undeveloped flower cluster, or the portion which is known as the scales of the involucre. They are boiled and served with drawn butter, but outside of France do not seem to be very generally appreciated. The plants are propagated first by seeds, sown in a hot-bed in March, and planted out at distances of from two to three feet. It is not always hardy enough for our winters in the northern states, though it proves so in all latitudes south of Washington. Here it is necessary on the approach of winter to draw the leaves together and earth up around them, and later to cover the tops with litter.

ARTICHOKE, JERUSALEM—(*Helianthus tuberosus.*)

This is an entirely different plant from the above, but as the two are sometimes confounded, we give engravings of both. The edible portion of this is the tuber, while that of the *Globe* Artichoke is the scales surrounding the flowers. The tubers of the Jerusalem Artichoke somewhat resemble the

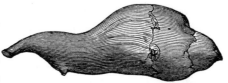

Fig. 70.—JERUSALEM ARTICHOKE.

potato in appearance, and the plant produces immense crops. But few persons in this country like the flavor, and it is rarely grown unless for stock or as a curiosity. Its culture is similar to the potato; it has stems, leaves, and flowers, much like the common sunflower.

BEAN, (*Phaseolus vulgaris* var. *nanus.*)—BUSH, SNAP, OR KIDNEY.

An indispensable vegetable, of easy cultivation, growing freely on almost any soil, though on well enriched land, it will be more prolific in quantity and more tender in quality. It is a plant of tropical origin, and like all such, should not be sown until the weather is settled and warm, and all danger from frost is past. In this latitude, the time of sowing should not be sooner than the 15th of May. Sow at intervals of two or three weeks, all through the season, if wanted for use. Seed may be sown in drills 18 to 24 inches apart, and three inches deep, dropping the seeds at distances of two or three inches in the drills, and covering to the general level. To such as use them all through the season, three or four quarts would be required, although a quart at one sowing would give an ample quantity for any average family.   The varieties most in use at present are *Early Valentine, Early China, Mohawk, Fejee, Black Wax,* and *Refugee.*

BEAN—POLE OR RUNNING, (*Phaseolus vulgaris*), AND LIMA, (*Phaseolus lunatus*).

Pole Beans are usually cultivated in hills three or four feet apart.   The poles, (which are best made of young cedar trees), should be nine or ten feet high, and firmly fixed at least eighteen inches deep in the ground, and the hills formed around them by digging up the soil and mixing it with a shovelful of well rotted manure, or an ounce or so of guano or bone-dust, if the stable manure is not attainable ; but in either case let the mixing be thorough.   The hills should be but two or three inches above the general level, and at least eighteen inches in diameter.   The term " hill " is an unfortunate one, as it often leads inexperienced persons to suppose that a tall heap must be made, and it is a common mistake to form miniature hills often a foot or more in hight, upon which to sow seeds or set plants ; the effect of this is to confine the roots to this small high and dry space.   When the word " hill " is used in this work, it is to indicate the place plants are to occupy, and unless some hight is mentioned, it is not above the general level.   After the hill has been properly formed around the pole, from five to six beans should be planted around it at a depth of two inches, but the planting should never be done in this latitude before the 20th of May.   In all our experience as seedsmen, we know of no seed that is so universally replanted as Lima Beans.   I think it safe to say, that at least half of all the people who buy, plant before the ground is dry and warm, and then tell us that the seed must have been bad, because it rotted in the ground.   In the hurry of business we have not always time to explain why they rotted, and would here state for the sake of ourselves and cotemporaries, that the reason why the Limas fail to grow in 99 cases out of 100, is, that they are planted too early, and that it is no fault of the seed, which is rarely imperfect. The proper method of planting Lima Beans is to push each one singly into the soil, with the eye downward ; the embryo is so very broad and flat that it is difficult for it to turn itself as smaller seeds do when placed in a wrong position.

The Large White Lima is the variety that is most prized.

The Giant Wax makes pods nine inches in length, and is a very productive variety.

The London Horticultural is used as snaps or shelled.

The Scarlet Runner is a highly ornamental variety, producing dazzling scarlet flowers during the whole summer. It is used mainly as a snap bean. Lima Beans are usually only planted once in this latitude, as they take nearly the whole season to mature. From thirty to fifty poles are sufficient for ordinary use; this will require from one to two quarts of seed.

BEET, (*Beta vulgaris.*)

Sow in shallow drills twelve to eighteen inches apart in April or May, dropping the seeds so that they will fall an inch or so apart. When the plants have grown to the hight of about two inches, thin out, so that they will stand four inches apart. When the roots are three inches in diameter, they are fit for use. Of course they are used when much larger, but the younger they are, the more delicate and tender. The varieties cultivated are limited to a few :

Early Egyptian.—A round, deep red variety, is the earliest.

Early Bassano.—A light salmon colored variety.

Fig. 71.—EGYPTIAN BEET.

Early Blood Turnip. —Later than either of the above, but best for general crop.

Long Smooth Red.— A long variety, best for winter use. About six ounces of seed will give 300 feet of row; enough for ordinary use unless succession crops are wanted, then double the quantity will be required.

BORECOLE OR KALE,
(*Brassica oleracea var.*)

The rather indefinite name of "sprouts" is given to this vegetable about New York. It is sown here in September, in rows one foot apart, treated in every way as spinach, and is ready for use in early spring. Four ounces of seed is sufficient to sow 300 feet of row. Two varieties of this, but little grown here, are the "Scotch Kale," or "Curled Greens," and the "Dwarf German Greens." The former is of a deep green color, the latter bluish purple, both varieties are much curled, almost like parsley. The seeds of these are sown in May, and transplanted in July, just as we do late cabbages, at distances of two feet apart each way. These "Greens," of either variety, when touched by frost, are the most tender and delicate of all the cabbage tribe, and it has always been a matter of wonder to me, why their cultivation has not been more general in this country. In Britain they are used very extensively as a winter vegetable. The most popular German variety is *Purple Borecole*. The most popular English variety is *Cottager's Kale*, very hardy and profitable, more weight being grown of it in the same space than of any other variety.

BROCCOLI, (*Brassica oleracea var.*)

We persist in growing under the two distinct names of Broccoli and Cauliflower, plants which at best are nothing more than very nearly related varieties. The main difference between them is, that what we call Broccoli, is planted for fall use, while that which we call Cauliflower is planted for spring or summer use ; though in this respect they are frequently reversed without seeming to mind it. For fall use the seed should be sown in the early part of May, which will give plants large enough to be set out in July. Further south the sowing of the seed should be delayed from four to six weeks later, and the plants be set out correspondingly later. Here we put them out in July, though further south it may be delayed to August or September. In the mild autumn weather of those latitudes this vegetable may be had in perfection from November to March, while with us, if planted out in July it matures during October and November. The plants are set at two and a half to three feet apart, and as a hundred plants are all that most families would use, it is cheaper to buy them, if in a section where they are sold, than to raise the plants from seed. It requires an abundance of manure. The varieties are :

White and Purple Cape.—There is no difference in

flavor, though the white is the most pleasant looking vegetable when cooked.

BRUSSELS SPROUTS, (*Brassica oleracea var.*)

This vegetable, as the engraving shows, is a variety of the cabbage which forms scarcely any terminal bud or head, but the buds along the stem, which in the ordi-

Fig. 72.—BRUSSELS SPROUTS.

nary cabbage remain small, are in this developed into small heads, which are the edible portion. This is much more used in Europe than with us; though it is not sufficiently hardy to endure our northern winters, it will stand in our latitude until Christmas. Its cultivation is exactly similar in all respects to that of Broccoli, except that it may be planted closer, say from one and a half to two feet apart.

CAULIFLOWER, (*Brassica oleracea var.*)

There is quite an ambition among amateur gardeners to raise early cauliflower, but as the conditions necessary to success with this are not quite so easy to command as with most other vegetables, probably not one in three

Fig. 73.—CAULIFLOWER.

who try it succeed. In England, and most places on the continent of Europe, it is the most valued of all vegetables, and is grown there nearly as easily as early cabbages. But it must be remembered that the temperature there is on the average ten degrees lower at the time it matures, (June), than with us ; besides their atmosphere is much more humid, two conditions essential to its proper development. I will briefly state how early cauliflowers can be most successfully grown here. First, the soil must be well broken, and pulverized by spading to at least a foot in depth, mixing through it a layer of three or four

inches of strong, well rotted, stable manure. The plants
may be either those from seed sown last fall and
wintered over in cold frames, or else started from
seeds sown in January or February, in a hot-bed or
greenhouse, and planted in small pots or boxes, so
as to make plants strong enough to be set out as
soon as the soil is fit to work, which in this latitude
is usually the first week in April. We are often applied
to for cauliflower plants as late as May, but the chances
of their forming heads when planted in May, are slim
indeed. The surest way to secure the heading of cauliflowers is to use what are called hand-glasses, some of
which are described in the chapter on Implements.
These are usually made about two feet square, which
gives room enough for three or four plants of cauliflower,
until they are so far forwarded that the glass can be taken
off. When the hand-glass is used, the cauliflowers may
be planted out in any warm border early in March and covered by them. This covering protects them from frosts
at night, and gives the necessary increase of temperature
for growth during the cold weeks of March and April ;
so that by the first week in May, if the cauliflower has
been properly hardened off by ventilating, (by tilting up
the hand-glasses on one side), they may be taken off
altogether, and then used to forward tomatoes, melons,
or cucumbers, at which date these may be started, if
under the protection of hand-glasses. If the weather is
dry, the cauliflowers will be much benefitted by being
thoroughly soaked with water twice or thrice a week ;
not a mere sprinkling, which is of no use, but a complete
drenching, so that the water will reach to the lowest
roots. Those planted later are set out and treated in the
same manner as cabbages. The two best varieties of
cauliflower we have found as yet, are the *Dwarf Erfurt*
and *Early Paris.*

CABBAGE, (*Brassica oleracea var.*)

The cabbage is so easily raised that but little space need be devoted to it here; like all of its tribe, it requires an abundance of manure for its full development. The early varieties should be either raised in cold-frames or in hot-beds, as stated for cauliflower, and planted out at distances of from twenty to thirty inches apart each way,

Fig. 74.—CABBAGE—EARLY WINNINGSTADT.

Fig. 75.—CABBAGE—SAVOY.

as early as the ground is fit to work in April. The best

early varieties are Early Summer, Early Wakefield, Early York, and Early Oxheart. As an intermediate variety the Winningstadt is very popular ; it has a sharply conical head, and sometimes grows quite large.

For late varieties, the seed should be sown in May, and the plants set out in July at two to three feet apart. For winter use the large Drumhead is usually grown, to the exclusion of all others, and while the Curled Savoy is vastly better flavored, not one Savoy is planted for every thousand Drumhead. The flavor of the Savoy is as superior to that of the Drumhead, as that of a Bartlett

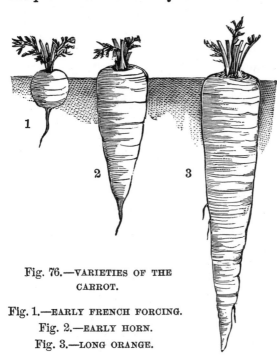

Fig. 76.—VARIETIES OF THE CARROT.

Fig. 1.—EARLY FRENCH FORCING.
Fig. 2.—EARLY HORN.
Fig. 3.—LONG ORANGE.

to that of a choke pear, and it is altogether the best late cabbage for family use.

CARROT, (*Daucus Carota.*)

Carrots are sown any time from April to June, in rows one foot apart, covering the seed two inches deep. If the soil is light, they will be better flavored. When the plants are an inch or so high, thin out to three or four inches apart. The varieties most in use are Early French Forcing, Early Horn and Long Orange. Eight ounces of seed will sow 300 feet of row, which, for most families, would be an abundance, both for summer and winter use. Carrots are much prized as food for horses and cows, and if wanted for this purpose in quantity, they should be sown with a seed-drill, in rows one and a half to two feet apart; about four pounds of seed per acre is required.

CELERY, (*Apium graveolens.*)

If I am fitted to instruct on the cultivation of any vegetable, it is this, as for many years I have cultivated nearly half a million roots annually, and this experience has resulted in greatly simplifying the operation. The seeds are sown on a well pulverized rich border, as early in the season as the ground can be worked. The bed is kept clear of weeds until July, when the plants are set out for the crop. But as the seedling plants are rather troublesome to raise, the small number wanted for private use, can usually be purchased cheaper than they can be raised on a small scale, (they rarely cost more than $1 per 100), and if they can be procured fresh from the market gardeners in the neighborhood, it is never worth while to sow the seed. The European plan is to make a trench six or eight inches deep, in which to plant celery, but our violent rain storms in summer soon showed us that this plan was not a good one here, so we set about planting on the level surface of the ground, just as we do with all vegetables. Celery is a " gross feeder," and requires an abundance of manure, which, as usual, must be well mixed and incorporated with the soil, before the celery is set out. When the ground is well prepared, we stretch a line to the distance required, and beat it slightly with a spade, so that it leaves a mark to show where to place the plants. These are set out at distances of six inches between the plants, and usually four feet between the rows. Great care must be taken in put-

ting out the celery, to see that the plant is set just to
the depth of the roots, if much deeper, the "heart"
might be too much covered up, which would impede the
growth.   It is also important that the soil be well packed
to the root in planting, and if the operation can be done
in the evening, and the plants copiously watered, no
farther attention will be required.

If planted in July, nothing is to be done but keep the
crop clear of weeds until September; by that time the
handling process is to be begun, which consists in drawing the earth to each side of the celery, and pressing it

Fig. 77.—" HANDLING " CELERY.

tightly to it, so as to give the leaves an upward growth
preparatory to blanching for use.   Supposing this handling process is done by the middle of September, by the
first week in October it is ready for " banking up," which
is done by digging the soil from between the rows and
laying or banking it up on each side of the row of celery;
after being so banked up in October, it will be ready for
use in three or four weeks if wanted at that time.   But
if, as is usually the case, it is needed for winter use only,
and is to be put away in trenches, or in the cellar, as
will be hereafter described, all that it requires is the
operation of "handling."   If the celery is to be left in
the open ground where it was grown, then a heavy bank

must be made on each side of the rows, and as cold weather approaches—say in this latitude by the middle of November—an additional covering of at least a foot of leaves or litter, must be closely packed against the bank. to protect it from frost.

Perhaps the best way to keep celery for family use, is in a cellar ; this can be done by storing it in narrow boxes, of a depth a little less than the hight of the celery. A few inches of sand or soil is placed in the bottom of the box, and the celery is packed upright ; the roots being placed on the sand at the bottom, none being put

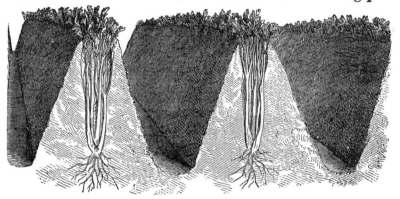

Fig. 78.—" BANKING UP " CELERY.

between the heads. Boxes thus packed and placed in a cool cellar in November, will be blanched fit for use during January, February, and March, though for succession, it will be better to put it in the boxes from the open ground at three different times, say October 25th, November 10th, and November 20th. Or if boxes are not at hand, the celery may be put away on the floor of the cellar in strips of nine or ten inches wide, separated by spaces of the same width, divided by boards of a width equal to the hight of the celery. The reason for dividing the celery in these narrow strips by boards, is to prevent the heating. which would take place if placed together in too thick masses. The dates above given

9

apply, of course, to the latitude of New York; if further south, do the work later; if further north, earlier. If one has no suitable cellar, the celery can be very readily preserved in the manner followed by market gardeners.

After it has been "handled" or straightened up, as before described, what is intended for use by Christmas, should be dug up by about October 25th; that to be used in January and February, by November 10th, and that for March use, by November 20th, which latter date is as late as it can be risked here; although it will stand quite a sharp frost, the weather by the end of November is

Fig. 79.—STORING CELERY IN TRENCHES FOR WINTER.

often severe enough to kill it, or so freeze it in the ground that it cannot be dug up. The ground in which it is to be preserved for winter use, must be as dry as possible, and so arranged that no water can remain in the trench. Dig a trench as narrow as possible, (it should not be wider than ten inches), and of a depth equal to the hight of the celery, that is, if the plant of celery be eighteen inches high, the trench should be dug eighteen inches deep. The celery is then packed exactly in the manner described for storing in boxes to be placed in the cellar; that is, stand it as near upright as possible, and pack as closely together as can be done without bruising it. As the weather becomes cold, the trenches should be gradually covered with leaves or litter, to the thickness of six or eight inches, which will be enough to prevent severe freezing, and enable the roots to be taken out easily when wanted. Fig. 79 represents this method of storing celery in trenches for winter use.

From 200 to 500 roots is the number usually required by an ordinary family. The varieties we recommend, are the Sandringham White and Dwarf Red. The red is as yet but little used in this country, though the flavor is better, and the plant altogether hardier than the white.

CELERIAC, OR TURNIP-ROOTED CELERY, (*Apium graveolens* var.)

Is grown almost the same as the common celery, and as it requires but little earthing-up, the rows may be nearer together. Its tur-

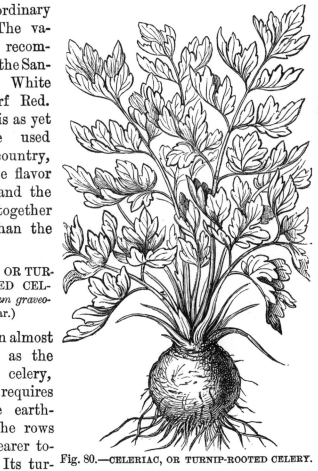

Fig. 80.—CELERIAC, OR TURNIP-ROOTED CELERY.

nip-like root is used as a salad, mostly by the French and Germans. It is sometimes stewed, but usually simply boiled, sliced, and dressed as a salad for the table.

CORN-SALAD OR FETTICUS, (*Fedia olitoria.*)

This is sold to a considerable extent in spring in the city markets for use as an early salad. For mode of cultivation, etc., see Spinach, as it is grown in exactly the same manner.

Fig. 81.—CORN-SALAD.

CHIVES, (*Allium Schœnoprasum.*)

An entirely hardy onion - like plant, of easy culture ; it will grow on almost any soil for years, without being transplanted. The leaves are the part used, and may be shorn off every two weeks during summer. It is propagated by tearing to pieces the old clumps and setting the divisions in rows a foot apart.

CRESS OR PEPPER GRASS, (*Lepidium sativum.*)

A spring and summer salad plant ; sow in early spring, and in succession, every week or so if desired, in rows one foot apart. The curled variety is the best, as it can be used for garnishing, as well as for salad.

CRESS-WATER, (*Nasturtium officinale.*)

A hardy aquatic plant, which can only be properly cultivated where there are running streams. If there is a brook on the place, all that would be wanted for private use may be had by setting a few plants or sowing seeds in spring on the margin of the water.

CORN, (*Zea Mays.*)

The varieties known as "Sweet," are the kinds cultivated to be used in the green state. Corn may either be planted in "hills," dropping three or four seeds in a hill four feet apart each way, or in rows five feet apart, dropping the seeds at distances of eight or ten inches in the rows. In this latitude it is useless to plant corn before the middle of May. For succession crops it should be planted every two or three weeks until July first; after that date it will not mature here. Corn requires a rich light soil to be early. The leading varieties are Dwarf Early Sugar for first early, Crosby's Early Sugar for second, and Stowell's Evergreen for main crops. Three or four quarts is required, if succession crops are sown; if only one crop, two or three pints will be sufficient.

CUCUMBER, (*Cucumis sativus.*)

In most places where the Cucumber is grown out-doors, it is more or less troubled with the "Striped Bug," but if only a few dozen hills are cultivated, it is not a very troublesome matter to pick them off, which is about the only sure way to get rid of them. The safest method of raising cucumbers, however, is to cover the seeds when first sown, with the hand-glass described in chapter on Implements; which by the time they are wanted for cucumbers, are no longer needed over cauliflowers. If such hand-glasses are not obtainable, a simple method is to use a light box ten or twelve inches square, to place over the seeds after sowing, covering it with a pane of

Fig. 82.

BRYANT'S PLANT PROTECTOR.

glass; this will not only forward the germination of the seeds, but will protect the plants against the bugs, until they are strong enough not to be injured by them. Bryant's Plant Protector, a simple article, made of light strips of wood, covered by mosquito netting, may be used instead of a hand-glass. This will be found equally valuable for protecting all plants liable to the attacks of flying insects, and against the light frosts, so often injurious to tender plants. Light, sandy soil is rather best for cucumbers ; the "hills" should be prepared in the same manner as for Lima Beans, but set three feet apart, dropping five or six seeds in each hill. Cucumbers may be sown about the middle of May, and in succession, every three or four weeks, until July. The White Spine and Long Green Prickly are favorite varieties. The Gherkin or Burr is by some used for pickling.

EGG PLANT, (*Solanum Melongena.*)

This is always an interesting vegetable to cultivate, being worthy of a place as an ornamental plant, as well as being much prized for culinary use. It is a native of the Tropics, and peculiarly tender. We find the seeds will not germinate freely under a temperature of seventy degrees ; and even then, often tardily, unless the conditions are just right. Nothing suits them so well as a warm hot-bed, and to get plants of the proper size to be set in the open ground by the end of May, the seeds should be sown early in March, and the plants potted into small pots when an inch or so in hight. But as only a dozen or two plants are needed for a family, whenever the plants

Fig. 83.—EGG PLANT.

can be purchased conveniently, it is never worth the trouble to attempt the raising of them from seeds, unless indeed there is room in a hot-bed, or hot-house used for other purposes. Do not plant out sooner than the 25th of May, unless they can be protected by hand-glasses. Set at distances of four feet apart, preparing the hills as described for Lima Beans. Each plant should average a dozen fruits, which will weigh from ten to forty ounces each. The best flavored variety in our opinion is the Black Pekin, but the most prolific is the New York Market. A pure pearly white variety is highly ornamental, and also of excellent flavor. The Egg Plant is usually fried in slices, but there are other methods to be found in the proper authorities in such matters.

ENDIVE, (*Cichorium Endivia.*)

A plant related to the lettuce. If sown in early spring, either in hot-bed or in the open ground, in April, it will be ready in May. Set out at distances of fifteen inches apart. It is mostly used towards fall, however, and when wanted at that time, should be sown in June or July, and set out in August and September; nothing further is done after planting but hoeing to keep down the weeds, until it attains its full growth, which is from twelve to eighteen inches in diameter. It is then "blanched," either by gathering up the leaves and tying them by their tops in a conical form, or by placing a slate, or flat stone, on the plant to exclude the light and effect the blanching. It is used as a salad. The varieties are the Moss Curled and Plain-leaved Batavian.

HERBS—SWEET.

Thyme, Sage, Basil, Sweet Marjoram, and Summer Savory are those in general use; the seeds of all except the last named, should be sown in shallow drills, one foot apart in May, and the plants will be fit for use in September and October.　Summer Savory does better if the seeds are sown where the plants are to grow.

GARLIC, (*Allium sativum.*)

Is used mostly by Europeans ; it grows freely on any soil ; the sets, obtained by breaking up the old bulbs, are planted in early spring in rows one foot apart, and five or

Fig. 84.—GARLIC BULBS.　　　Fig. 85.—HORSERADISH ROOT.

six inches between the plants.　When the leaves wither, the bulbs are taken up and hung in a dry, cool place.

HORSERADISH, (*Nasturtium Armoracia.*)

For family use a few roots of this should be planted in some out-of-the-way corner of the vegetable garden ; a dozen roots, once planted, will usually give enough for a life-time, as it increases and spreads so that there is never any danger of being without it ; the trouble is, if it is once admitted into the garden, it is difficult to be got rid of if so desired.

KOHLRABI, OR TURNIP-ROOTED CABBAGE, (*Brassica oleracea* var.)

This vegetable resembles a turnip, but is regarded as a variety of the cabbage, with a fleshy edible stem. Seeds should be sown in rows fifteen or eighteen inches apart, in May or June, and when an inch high, thinned out to nine or ten inches. It is a favorite vegetable with the Germans, and immense quantities are sold in the

Fig. 86.—KOHLRABI.

markets of New York in the fall. There are two varieties, White and Purple.

LEEK, (*Allium Porrum*.)

Sow in April, and plant out in June or July, in rows one foot apart and six inches between the plants. It is used mainly during the winter months; it is an entirely hardy plant, yet in order that it

Fig. 87.—LEEK.

may be handy to get at in winter, it is better to put it in trenches, as advised for preserving celery.

LETTUCE, (*Lactuca sativa.*)

Lettuce should be sown in a hot-bed or greenhouse if wanted early ; seeds sown there in February will give nice plants to set out in April, to mature in May, or if it is sown in the open ground in April and planted out in May, it will mature in June, and so on through the summer season if succession crops are desired, as it only takes from five to six weeks to mature. The great excellence of lettuce consists in its freshness, and it can rarely be purchased in perfect condition ; hence, those who would enjoy it in its best state should raise it themselves.

For early use, to be ready in May, the Curled Silesia and Boston Market are the best ; while for summer use, the Curled India and Plain Drumhead should be sown, as they do not readily run to seed. The Cos varieties are mainly used in Europe, and are by far the best flavored ; but from their tendency to run to seed in our warmer climate, are but little cultivated, though they might be safely grown in the cool weather, in spring, or in fall. An ounce of seed of each variety will be ample.

MARTYNIA, (*Martynia proboscidea.*)

The unripe pods taken when perfectly tender, are used for pickling. They must be gathered every day or two, or some will become hard and useless. Sow in open ground in May, and transplant to two feet each way in June.

MELON, MUSK, (*Cucumis Melo.*)

The cultivation of the Melon is almost identical with that of the cucumber, to which reference may be made.

The varieties are numerous, those named below are the most popular.

Green Citron.—Medium size, deeply netted, almost round in shape, flesh green, delicious flavor.

White Japan.—A distinct and white - skinned sort, flesh yellow, richly flavored.

Ispahan. — A valuable variety for the southern states, but too late to mature in the north. It grows to upwards of a foot in length; skin, when fully ripe, light yellow; flesh yellowish-white, with a rich perfume and flavor. *Cassaba* is a related variety, and in most seasons ripens with us.

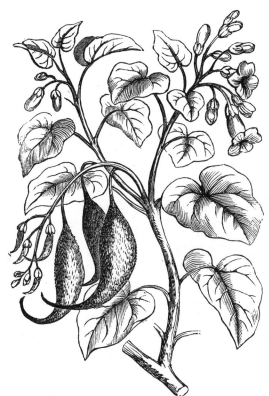

Fig. 88.—MARTYNIA.

Ward's Nectar and *Skillman's Netted*, are among the best for the family garden.

MELON, WATER, (*Citrullus vulgaris.*)

The cultivation of the Water Melon is in all respects similar to that of the Musk Melon, except that being a larger and stronger growing plant, it requires to be planted at greater distances. The hills should not be less than eight feet apart each way. It delights in light sandy soil, and will not grow satisfactorily on heavy, clayey soils. The leading sorts are :

Mountain Sprout.—A large-sized, red-fleshed variety, of excellent flavor.

Phinney's Early.—Flesh of a deep red, very sweet.

Fig. 89.—WATER-MELON—PHINNEY'S EARLY.

Ice Cream.—A white-fleshed variety, and one of the earliest; best to be grown in northern or eastern states.

Orange.—So called because the flesh parts readily from the rind when ripe. The flesh is red, and rather coarse ; it keeps longer than any other.

Rattlesnake, also called *Joe Johnson,* is a fine variety for the southern states, and is largely grown for shipment to the northern markets.

MUSTARD, (*Sinapis alba.*)

For use and cultivation see Cress.

MUSHROOM, (*Agaricus campestris.*)

Many who have a taste for horticultural pursuits grow mushrooms as much for the novelty of the thing as for the use, for it is certainly very gratifying for an amateur to find that he has succeeded with a crop of this curious vegetable in mid-winter, when everything outside is frost-locked and snow-bound. I have said that the novelty is attractive, for in growing all other plants the cultivator sees something tangible to start with, either seeds, plants, or roots, but with the mushroom it may be said he sees neither, for no seeds can be discovered either with the naked eye or with a magnifier, and it requires some faith to believe the minute thread-like substance we call " spawn," to be either plants or roots.

Mushrooms are always raised in the dark, and any cellar, stable, or an out-house of any sort, wherein a temperature of 45° to 65° can be commanded, will grow them. There are various methods followed by mushroom growers, but I will only give one, premising that if the directions given are strictly followed, success is just as certain as in growing a crop of peas or potatoes. Let horse droppings be procured from the stables each day, in quantities not less than a barrow load ; to every barrow load of droppings, add half the quantity of fresh loam, from a pasture or sod land, or soil of any kind that has not been manured, (the objection to old manured soil being that it may contain the spores of spurious fungi.) Let the droppings and soil be mixed together day by day, as the manure can be procured ; or if they can be had all at once in sufficient quantity, so much the better. Let the heap, (which should be under cover), be turned every day, so that it is not allowed to heat violently until you have got together a sufficient quantity to form a bed of the desired size. From the prepared droppings and soil, begin to form the bed. A convenient width is four feet, and the length may be as great as desired. First spread a thin layer of the compost, pounding it down firmly with a brick or mallet, layer after layer, until it reaches a depth of eight inches. Be careful that the thickness is just about eight inches, as if more, it would heat too violently, and if less, it would not heat enough. Into this bed plunge a thermometer; in two or three days the bed will heat, so that the thermometer will rise to 100° or over. As soon as the temperature declines to 90°, take a sharp stick and make holes an inch or so in diameter all over the bed, at about a foot apart, and six inches deep ; into these holes drop two or three pieces of "spawn," and cover up the hole again with the compost of which the bed is made, and beat it slightly again, so that the bed will present the same level surface as before the spawn was put in. Let the bed remain in this condition for ten or twelve days, by which time the spawn will have run all through it. Now spread evenly over the surface of the bed about two inches of fresh loam, press it down moderately with the back of a spade, and cover up the bed with hay or straw to the thickness of three or four inches. If this operation is finished in November or December, and the place has an average temperature of 55°, you may look out for a crop in January or February. The bed will continue bearing about three or four weeks, and the crop is usually enormous, often producing a bushel on two square yards of space. After the first crop is gathered, a second, and even a third, can be taken if desired, from the same bed without further trouble than to spread a little fresh soil on the surface, giving it a gentle watering and covering up with hay as before. Great care must be taken that after placing the spawn in the newly made bed, the earth covering is not put on sooner than ten or twelve days ; in my first attempt at mushroom growing, I failed two years in succession, because I put on the soil when the spawn was first put into the bed ; by so doing, the steam arising from the manure was prevented from passing off, and the result was, that the spawn rotted. I believe this very common error is the cause of most of the failures in raising mushrooms.

NASTURTIUM—INDIAN CRESS, (*Tropæolum majus.*)

A highly ornamental plant, cultivated in flower-gardens as well as in the kitchen garden. The shoots and flowers are sometimes used in salads, but it is mainly grown for its fruit or seed pods, which are pickled in vinegar and used as a substitute for capers. The plant is of the easiest culture. Sow in shallow drills in May. The *tall* variety will reach a hight of ten or fifteen feet if furnished with strings or wires, and makes an excellent screen for shade, or for quickly covering up and conceal-

Fig. 90.—OKRA.

ing any unsightly place. The *dwarf* variety is grown like peas, and staked with brush.

OKRA OR GUMBO, (*Abelmoschus esculentus.*)

A vegetable of the easiest culture. Sow in drills in May, three feet apart for dwarf, and four feet for tall sorts, in drills two or three inches deep. The long pods when very young and tender, are used in soups, stews, etc., and are very nutritious.

ONION, (*Allium cepa.*)

Onions are raised either by "sets," which are small dry onions grown the previous year, or from seeds. When grown from the sets, they should be planted out as early in spring as the ground is dry enough to work ; plant them in rows one foot apart, with sets three or four inches apart. When raised from sets, the onions can be used in the green state in June, or they will be ripened off by July. When raised from seeds, these are sown at about the same distance between the rows, and when the young plants are an inch or so high, they are thinned out to two or three inches apart. It is important that onion-seed be sown very early. In this latitude it should be sown not later than the middle of April, for if delayed until May, warm weather sets in and delays, or rather prolongs the growth until fall, and often the bulbs will not ripen ; we find that unless the onion-tops dry off and the bulbs ripen by August, they will hardly do so later. The best known sorts are White Portugal or Silver Skinned, Yellow Dutch or Strasburg, and Wethersfield Red.

Two kinds are grown exclusively from bulbs ; one of these is the Potato Onion, or " Multipliers," which increase by the bulb splitting up and dividing itself into six or eight smaller bulbs, which in turn form the sets to plant for the next crop. The other variety is what is called "Top Onion," which forms little bulbs on the stem in the place of flowers ; these are in clusters, and about the size of hazel nuts. These small bulbs are broken apart and planted in spring at the same distances as the "sets" referred to above ; all mature in August.

PARSLEY, (*Carum Petroselinum.*)

But a very small quantity of this is usually wanted in the family garden. Sow in shallow drills in April or

May. A good plan is to sow in shallow boxes as much as may be needed ; they can be placed wherever there is moderate light, and no frost ; by this means a fresh supply may be kept on hand in hard winter weather, when it is most desirable to have it, either for garnishing dishes or for other uses. The best variety to grow is the Moss, or Double Curled.

PARSNIP, (*Pastinaca sativa.*)

For mode of cultivation of parsnips, see carrot, as their culture is identical, except that this being hardy, can be left out in winter, while in this latitude carrots cannot. A portion of the crop may be dug and stored in the cellar or in trenches, and the remainder may be left until spring. The *Hollow Crowned* is best for general use.

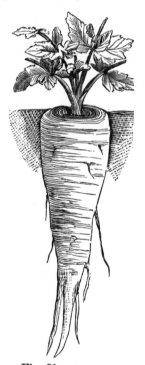

Fig. 91.—PARSNIP.

PEA, (*Pisum sativum.*)

The pea is indispensable in the garden, and there is more satisfaction in growing it on one's own ground, than there is in raising any other vegetable. If too old when picked, or stale, which is too often the case when purchased from the dealers, peas have but little resemblance to those taken directly from the vines. For an early crop peas should be one of the first things sown in the spring. We prefer to sow in double rows, which saves half the labor in staking or bushing up, and gives nearly the same crop to the row as if sown in single rows. Double rows are made at eight or nine inches apart, and four feet from other rows. Set a line and draw the drills with a hoe three or four inches deep; the seed should be sown to lay as near as possible an inch or so apart. The Sidney Seed-Sower, mentioned in the chapter on Implements, is a most convenient affair for sowing peas; one can with a few minutes practice distribute the seed with great regularity. In order to have a succession of crops of peas, they should be sown every two or three weeks until July. If succession crops are grown, an average quantity for a family would be twelve quarts; if only first crops of early and late, from four to six quarts will be sufficient.

The varieties of peas are almost innumerable, and new sorts—or at least sorts with new names—are sent out every year. They may be classed in two groups, the round and the wrinkled peas. The round varieties are the earliest, but they are as much inferior to the wrinkled or marrow kinds, as field is to sweet corn; these two groups are subdivided according to hight. The earliest pea is *Daniel O'Rourke*, under some of its dozen or more names, for most of the "early" and "extra early" peas are only selected strains of this, which, under other names, dates back into the last century. It is of medium hight, productive, and valuable as yielding the earliest crops. The earliest of the wrinkled sorts is the *Alpha*, of medium hight. The standard late sort is the *Champion of England*, an old variety, which has not yet been superseded. The dwarf sorts, which grow only about a foot high and need no brush, are very handy in the family garden, as they may be used to occupy odd spaces. The leading dwarfs are *Tom Thumb*, early but round, and *Little Gem*, productive and of the best quality. The catalogues give the merits of numerous other sorts, early, medium, and late.

PEPPER, or CAPSICUM, (*Capsicum annuum.*)

The Pepper is sown and cultivated in all respects the same as the Egg-Plant, which may be referred to. The varieties are the Bull-Nose, or Bell, and the Cayenne.

POTATO, (*Solanum tuberosum.*)

Potatoes are grown by planting the tubers, either cut or whole, it makes but little difference which; if large, cut them; if small, leave them uncut. They are usually planted in drills three feet apart, and four or five inches deep. The ground should be prepared by first spreading in the drills a good coat of stable manure, say two inches deep, upon which are planted the tubers or sets, at distances of eight or ten inches apart. In a warm exposure planting may be begun early in April, and the crop will be fit for use in June. Some of the small-leaved varieties such as the Ash-leaved Kidney, were formerly grown under hand glasses, or in frames, to forward them, but now this is hardly worth the trouble, as our supplies from southern latitudes are so early that it is no longer desirable to force the crop. The generally favorite variety for early crops is still the Early Rose; and for general crop, Peach-Blows; but there are scores of other varieties, which have a special or local reputation.

PUMPKIN, (*Cucurbita Pepo.*)

Pumpkins are still grown in many gardens with a tenacity that is astonishing, when it should long ago have been known that they have no business there, as their first cousins, the squashes, are eminently superior for every culinary purpose whatever. The Pumpkin is a valuable product for the farm, as a food for cattle, but for nothing else. If people will waste valuable land in raising pumpkins, they may plant them the same as directed for squashes.

RADISH, (*Raphanus sativus.*)

One of the first vegetables that we crave in spring is the Radish, and it is so easy of culture that every family can have it fresh, crisp, and in abundance. The smallest garden patch of a few feet square, will give enough for a family. It is sown either in drills or broadcast, care being taken that the seed is not put in too thickly ; from one to two inches apart either in drill or broadcast, being the proper distance, as usually every seed germinates. The best varieties are the Red and French Turnip, and the Short Top Long, Red, or White. If wanted specially early, the above sorts are best for hot-bed forcing ; for summer and winter use the yellow and gray varieties are preferred.

RHUBARB OR PIE PLANT, (*Rheum Rhaponticum.*)

Rhubarb may be planted in either fall or spring, using either plants raised from the seed, or sets obtained by divisions of the old roots, taking care to have a bud to each. Set at distances of three or four feet apart each way. The place where each plant is to be set, should be dug eighteen inches deep and the same in width, and the soil mixed with two or three shovelfuls of well-rotted stable manure. Two dozen strong plants will be enough for the wants of an average family. If desired in winter or early spring, a few roots can be taken up and placed in a warm cellar or any such dark and warm place. The roots, if the cellar is dark, may be put in a box with earth around them, or if in a light cellar, they may be put in the bottom of a barrel with earth, and the top covered. The only care needed is to see that the roots do not get too dry, and to water if necessary, when it will grow with but little care The useful portions is the long and thick leaf-stalks, and these when forced are much finer in flavor than when grown exposed to air and light in the open garden.　The plants in the open ground should have the flower-stalks cut away as they appear.

Fig. 92.—RHUBARB.

In gathering do not cut the leaf-stalks, as they will readily come away by a side-wise pull, and leave no remnant to decay.　The varieties are Myatt's Victoria and Linnæus.

SALSIFY, OR OYSTER PLANT, (*Tragapogon porrifolius.*)

The culture of this vegetable is the same in all respects as for carrots, which see.　Like the parsnip, it is hardy, and can be left out during winter in any district without injury from frost.　It is rapidly becoming more popular.

It is stewed like parsnips or carrots, is used to make soup,

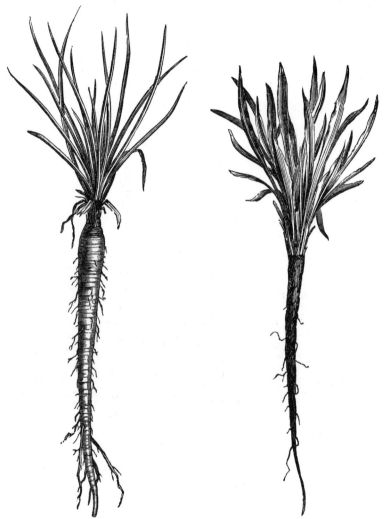

Fig. 93.—SALSIFY.   Fig. 94.—SCORZONERA.

which has a decided flavor of the oyster, or is first boiled
and then fried.   There is but one kind.

SCORZONERA—BLACK SALSIFY, (*Scorzonera Hispanica.*)

This is somewhat different in flavor from Salsify, and

is preferred to it by many ; it has much broader leaves, but it is cultivated and used in the same manner.

SEA KALE, (*Crambe maritima.*)

Sea Kale is a favorite vegetable in European gardens, but here, as yet, almost unknown. Anticipating that at no distant day it may be as generally cultivated as it deserves to be, I briefly describe the mode of culture. The seeds of Sea Kale should be sown in the greenhouse, or in a slight hot-bed in February or March, and when the plants are an inch or two in hight, they should be potted into two or three-inch pots and placed in a cold frame to harden, until sufficiently strong to be planted in the open ground. It should then be set out in rows three feet apart, with two feet between the plants, on land enriched as for any ordinary cabbage crop. If the plants and the soil in which they have been planted are both good, and cultivation has been properly attended to, by keeping the plants well hoed during the summer, it will have "crowns" strong enough to give a crop the

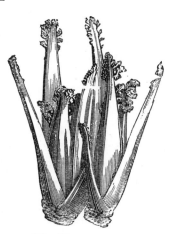

Fig. 95.—SEA KALE.

next season. In the northern states it will be necessary to cover the rows with three or four inches of leaves, to protect the plants from frost. Sea Kale is only fit for use when "blanched," and to effect this, on the approach of spring the "crowns" should be covered with some light material, such as sand or leaf-mold, to the depth of twelve or fifteen inches, so that the young shoot being thus excluded from the light, will become blanched in growing through this covering. Sometimes cans made

for the purpose, or large flower-pots, or even wooden
boxes, are inverted over the plants, the object in each
case being to exclude the light.   If it is desired to force
Sea Kale, or forward it earlier, the materials used to
make hot-beds, leaves or stable manure are heaped over
the pots or cans in a sufficient quantity to generate the
proper heat to forward or force on the growth of the
plants.   The young shoots are cut from the plant before
the leaves are developed, and when cooked, have a flavor
something between asparagus and cauliflower, but by
most persons much preferred to either.   The engraving
shows a young shoot when ready for the table.

SHALLOTS, (*Allium Ascalonicum.*)

A plant of the onion genus, which is cultivated by setting out the divided roots in September in rows a foot
apart, allowing six inches between them.   It is entirely
hardy, and fit for use in early spring.

SPINACH, (*Spinacia oleracea.*)

Spinach is a vegetable of easy culture.   It may either
be sown in spring or fall.   If in fall, the proper time is
from the 10th to the 25th of September, in rows one foot
apart ; sow rather thickly.   Cover the plants with two
or three inches of hay or leaves on the approach of severe
frost in December.   When sown in the fall, the crop of
course is ready for use much earlier than when sown in
spring, as half the growth is made in the fall months.
By the time the seed can be sown in spring, the crop that
has been wintered over will be coming into use.   To follow the crop thus wintered, seeds should be sown in the
same manner in spring, as early as the soil can be worked,
and another sowing may be made two weeks later.   The
round-seeded variety is best for winter sowing, and the
prickly seeded for spring.   About four ounces is enough
for ordinary wants for either season's sowing.

SPINACH, SUBSTITUTES FOR.

In the southern states, or even in our northern sum-

mers, Spinach runs rapidly to seed, if sown in hot weather, and several plants may be used as substitutes. Among these are Swiss Chard, a species of beet, sometimes called Spinach Beet, or Perpetual Spinach. Young plants of the ordinary beet are by some pre-

Fig. 96.—SWISS CHARD.

ferred to spinach; ordinarily beets need thinning, and the seed is sometimes sown very thickly, in order that there may be an abundance of thinnings to use as spinach, or beet greens; they are used with the young beet attached, which should not be thicker than an ordinary lead-pencil; if larger, the leaves will be too strong. Another substitute is

NEW ZEALAND SPINACH, (*Tetragonia expansa.*)

This is a remarkable plant, of low branching habit,

Fig. 97.—NEW ZEALAND SPINACH.

and grows with surprising luxuriance during hot

10

weather. Single plants often measure from five to eight feet in diameter. The leaves are used exactly as ordinary spinach. It should not be sown before warm weather sets in in May, and the plants should be set out in hills three or four feet apart each way.

SQUASH, (*Cucurbita Pepo and C maxima.*)

The summer varieties are, among others, the White and Yellow Bush and Summer Crookneck. As with

Fig. 98.—SQUASH—WHITE BUSH.

all plants of this class, it is useless to sow these before warm weather in May, and the directions given for cucumbers and melons, are alike applicable to the squash, except that the distances apart of the hills; these should

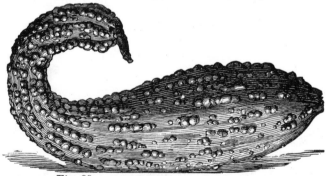

Fig. 99.—SQUASH—SUMMER CROOKNECK.

be from three to four feet for the bush sorts, and from six to eight for the other varieties which "run" or make a long vine. The fall or winter squashes are planted at the same time, but are allowed to mature or ripen, while the summer varieties are used green. They are usually planted eight or nine feet apart, in hills prepared in the usual way. These squashes are great feeders, and for the best results the soil should be well enriched, besides the special manuring in the hills, as the vines throw out roots at every joint to assist in feeding and maturing the heavy crop they usually bear. The popular varieties are

Fig. 100.—SQUASH—MARBLEHEAD.

Hubbard, Marblehead, Yokohama, and Winter Crookneck. Most of the winter varieties, if kept in a dry atmosphere at a temperature from forty to fifty degrees, will keep until May. A garret room in a moderately well heated dwelling house, will often be a very suitable place for storing them.

SWEET POTATO, (*Ipomœa Batatas.*)

It is useless to attempt to grow the Sweet Potato on anything but a light and dry soil. On clayey soils the plant not only grows poorly, but the potatoes raised upon such soil are watery, and poorly flavored. The plants are raised by laying the roots on their sides on a hot-bed or bench of a greenhouse, and covering them over with

sand, about the first week in May; by keeping up
an average temperature of 75° or 80°, fine plants will be
produced by June 1st, at which time they should be
planted in this vicinity. The plants are set in hills three
feet apart each way, or on
ridges four feet apart, and
12 or 15 inches between
the plants, drawing the
earth up to them as they
grow, until the top of the
ridge or hill is four or six
inches above the level.
The soil under the ridges
should be highly manured,
and as the vines grow they
should be kept clear of
weeds ; when late in the
season they show a dis-
position to root at the
joints, they must be
moved every week or so;
this is easily done by running a rake handle or
other stick under the vines
and lifting them sufficiently to draw out the small
roots upon the stem. As
is the case with many other
vegetables of which the
plants or sets are raised in

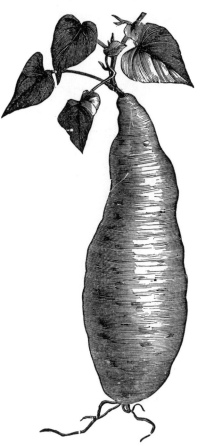

Fig. 101.—SWEET POTATO.

large quantities for sale, it is better and cheaper when
Sweet Potato plants are procurable, to purchase them,
than to attempt to raise the small number required in a
private garden. A hundred plants not costing more than
a dollar, are all that most families would require. The
Nansemond is the favorite variety.

TOMATO, (*Lycopersicum esculentum.*)

If any vegetable is grown in a family garden, it is almost certain to be the Tomato. Hundreds of people who have only a few feet of ground at their disposal, manage to cultivate a dozen or two of tomato-plants, though they may have nothing else ; so well is it known that I think few of my readers will require to be told much about its culture. The Tomato will grow anywhere, and under almost any circumstances, provided always that it has the necessary high temperature ; it is essentially a plant of the Tropics, and need never be sown in a hot-bed here before March, or planted in the open ground before the middle of May. When cultivated in private gardens, the tomato-vine should always be provided with some sort of trellis, or be tacked up against a fence or wall. By this treatment, not only will a heavier crop be obtained, but the flavor will be better ; when the fruit rests on the ground it has often an inferior flavor, particularly when eaten raw, and is also more apt to decay. A few dozen plants usually suffice for an ordinary family, and if there are no hot-beds or other glass arrangements on hand, the plants had better be purchased, as they are sold cheaply everywhere. The favorite varieties are the Trophy, Champion Cluster, and Conqueror.

TURNIP, (*Brassica campestris.*)

The Turnip, if wanted for an early crop, is sown in early spring, as directed for beets. The best sorts are the varieties known as White and Purple-top Strap-leaved and Yellow Aberdeen. If for winter or fall use, sowing should be deferred until July or August. The Ruta Baga or Swedes, being sown in July, and the earlier winter sorts, such as Yellow Globe or Flat Dutch, are sown in August.

GENERAL INSTRUCTIONS.

In concluding the section of this book devoted to vegetable growing, we will give a few general instructions
that may have been omitted in the details already given.
In sowing all kinds of seeds, more particularly those of
small size, be careful, if the soil is dry, to "firm" or
press down the surface of the bed or row after sowing,
with a light roller or back of a spade, more especially if
the weather is beginning to get warm. Crops are often
lost through the failure of the seeds to germinate, for
the simple reason that the soil is left loose about the tiny
seeds, and the dry atmosphere penetrates to them, shriv-
eling them up until all vitality is destroyed. Again for
the same reason, when setting out plants of any kind, be
certain that the soil is pressed close to the root. In our
large plantings in market gardening, particularly in summer, we make it a rule in dry weather to turn back on
the row after planting it with the dibber or trowel, and
press the earth firmly to each plant with the foot; we
have seen whole acres of celery and cabbage plants lost,
solely through neglect of this precaution. Never work
the soil while it is so wet as to clog, better wait a week
for it to dry than to stir it if wet. In no work in which
men are engaged is the adage, "A stitch in time saves
nine," more applicable than to the work of the farm or
garden. The instant that weeds appear, attack them
with the hoe or rake ; do not wait for them to get a
foot high, or a twelfth part of it, but break every inch of
the surface crust of the ground just so soon as a germ of
weed growth shows itself. And it will be better to do it
even before any weeds *show*, for by using a small sharp
steel rake, two or three days after your crop is planted
or sown, you will kill the weeds just as their seeds are
germinating. The newly developed germ of the strongest
weed is at that time very tender. In my market garden

operations I had one man whose almost exclusive duty it was to work in summer with the steel rake, and in a few days after a crop was planted, the surface was raked over, destroying the thousands of weeds just ready to appear. Had we waited for the weeds to be seen, so that they were too large to be destroyed by the raking, four men could not have done with the hoe the work accomplished by this man with the rake.

CHAPTER LI.

GARDEN IMPLEMENTS.

The tool-shed is an important and necessary appendage to a well kept garden. The following list includes such implements as are generally needed in private gardens :

THE WHEELBARROW, (Fig. 102).—The wheelbarrow is

Fig. 102.—GARDEN WHEELBARROW.

an important vehicle in the garden, for the moving of soils, carrying manures, and for conveying the products of the vegetable garden to the house or place of storage, and numerous other purposes. It may be purchased of different sizes and styles, or can be "home-made" by those possessing a little mechanical skill.

THE SPADE, (Fig. 103).—The uses of the spade in a garden are too obvious, and general, to need description. The best in use are Ames' cast-steel, which are light, strong, and durable, and work clean and bright.

THE SHOVEL, (Fig. 104).—The shovel is used for load‧ing, and for mixing and spreading composts and short manures. They are made with long or short handles.

THE DIGGING FORK, (Fig. 105), or Forking Spade, is used instead of a spade to dig in manures, to loosen the earth about the roots of trees, or for taking up root crops ; being less liable to cut or injure them than the spade. It is often

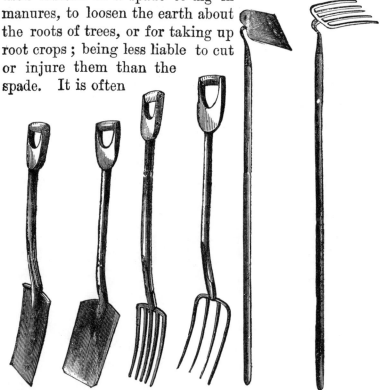

Fig. 103.   Fig. 104.   Fig. 105.   Fig. 106.   Fig. 107.   Fig. 108.

used instead of the spade, as by its aid the soil can be more readily broken and pulverized.

THE MANURE FORK, (Fig. 106).—Is made of cast-steel with from four to six prongs, and is used for mixing, loading, and spreading manures, work which could not be efficiently done without it.

THE COMMON OR DRAW HOE.—There are several patterns of draw hoes, but the one in general use is the common square hoe, as represented in fig. 107. Its uses in the garden are manifold, and it has frequently to do duty for several other implements. Its principle uses are to clean the surface of the ground from weeds, to open trenches for seeds, and to cover them.

THE PRONG HOE, (Fig. 108).—This is one of the most useful of all garden tools, and is far superior to the blade hoe for stirring and pulverizing the soil. It cannot, it is true, be used where weeds have been allowed to grow to any considerable hight, but then we claim that in all well regulated gardens, weeds should never be allowed to grow so large that they cannot be destroyed by the prong hoe.

THE DUTCH OR PUSH HOE, (Fig. 109), is sometimes preferred to the preceding for cutting the weeds between the rows of vegetables, a work which can be done very quickly by its aid ;

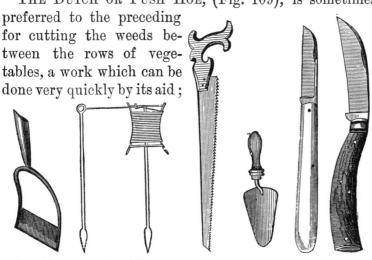

Fig. 109.   Fig. 110.   Fig. 111.   Fig. 112.   Fig. 113.

it is not so generally useful as the draw hoe, but is better for the special purposes of destroying weeds.

THE REEL AND LINE, (Fig. 110), are necessary in

every well regulated garden, enabling us to plant in straight and accurate rows. The line should be of strong hemp, and is wound upon the reel when not in use.

THE PRUNING SAW, (Fig. 111), is used for cutting off branches that are too large for the knife, for removing dead ones, etc. It can be had in various sizes, from fourteen to twenty inches in length.

THE GARDEN TROWEL, (Fig. 112), is used for setting the smaller kinds of plants when transferred from pots to the open ground; for transplanting annuals and many other uses, it is a very necessary little implement.

PRUNING AND BUDDING KNIVES, (Fig. 113), are necessary to every gardener. They are of different sizes and shapes, for the various purposes of grafting, budding, etc., and are made of the best steel.

GRAPE SCISSORS.—These are slender-pointed scissors, used for thinning out the berries of foreign grapes when

Fig. 114.—LAWN SCYTHE.

they are about half grown, so that those that are left may have room to develop. This operation should never be neglected if large berries and well shaped bunches are desired.

FLOWER GATHERERS.—A very useful article; the scissors cutting off, and at the same time holding fast the flower or fruit after it is cut, thus enabling one to reach much farther to cut flowers or fruits than if both hands had to be used. It is particularly useful in gathering rose-buds, as the stem can be cut off with but little danger from the thorns.

LAWN SCYTHES, (Fig. 114).—The lawn scythe is now but little used, the lawn mower taking its place, unless on hill-sides or among trees or shrubs, where the lawn mower cannot be worked.

LAWN MOWERS, (Fig. 115).—The great improvements made in Lawn Mowers during the past few years, and the low price at which they may now be obtained, have made their introduction common to every garden. They are of many sizes, from the small machine that can be easily worked by a boy,

Fig. 115.—LAWN MOWER.

and admirably adapted for city garden plots, to the large horse mowers, that may be daily seen in use in our larger parks. We have in use both the "Excelsior" and "Archimedean" Lawn Mowers, and have found them excellent in all respects.

THE GARDEN ROLLER, (Fig. 116), is indispensable to a well kept lawn, and should always follow after mowing, keeping the ground level and compact; and after gravel walks have been raked over, the roller is necessary to smooth them down.

THE WOODEN LAWN RAKE, (Fig. 117), is used for raking off lawns previous to and after using the scythe or lawn mower, and for removing dead leaves and other rubbish.

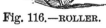

Fig. 116.—ROLLER.

THE RAKE, (Fig. 118), is used to level the surface of the ground after it has been spaded or hoed, and to prepare it for the reception of seeds or plants. Rakes are made of different sizes, for convenience in using between rows of plants, with from six to six-teen teeth. When a crop like cabbages is newly planted, we use the rake in preference to anything else, as raking over the surface before the weeds start to grow, destroys the germ of the weed, never allowing it to appear at all.

THE GRASS EDGING KNIFE, (Fig. 119), is used for cutting the grass edgings of flower-beds, its rounded edge fitting into curved lines, for which the spade would be unsuitable.

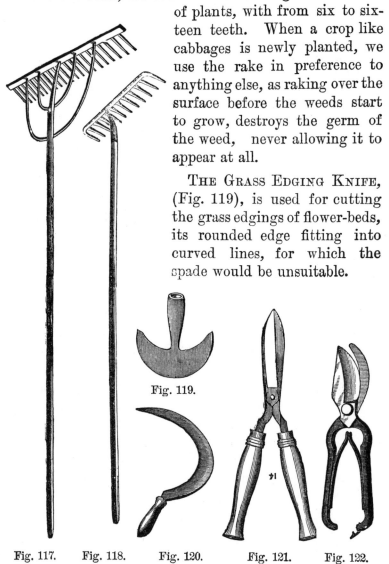

Fig. 119.

Fig. 117.   Fig. 118.   Fig. 120.   Fig. 121.   Fig. 122.

THE SICKLE, (Fig. 120).—This is a most useful imple-ment for switching around and trimming off grass, in places where the scythe or lawn mower cannot be used, or where the place to be cut is small.

HEDGE SHEARS, (Fig. 121), are better fitted for clipping hedges than the Bill Hook, sometimes used for the purpose, particularly in inexperienced hands. A line should be set at the hight to which the hedge is to be cut, as a guide to work by.

HAND-PRUNING SHEARS, (Fig. 122). —These are very efficient and useful; they will cut off a small branch as clean as if a knife had been used. They are indispensable in pruning small fruit-trees and vines, and for use in the grapery and garden.

POLE OR TREE PRUNING SHEARS, (Fig. 123). — These shears are attached to a pole, and operated by means of a lever moved by a cord or a wire; they enable one to cut off branches from trees, shrubbery, etc., that are beyond the reach of the ordinary pruning shears.

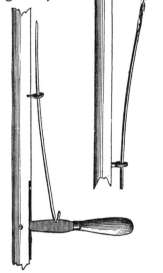

Fig. 123.—TREE PRUNER.

Branches of an inch and a half in diameter may be easily cut off with this instrument.

GARDEN SYRINGE, (Fig. 124).—The syringe is in

Fig. 124.—GARDEN SYRINGE.

daily use in the greenhouse or conservatory, where syringing is necessary to keep the plants in a flourishing

and healthy condition. They are made of several sizes
and patterns, and fitted with roses for dispersing water
with varying force.

WATERING-POT.—A watering-pot is indispensable in
the greenhouse or conservatory,
where it is daily needed. It
should be obtained of a suitable size, from one to four gallons, with a rose for sprinkling,
which may be detached at will.

THE EXCELSIOR PUMP, (Fig.
125), is a very compact and useful implement for greenhouse
and garden work. It is easily
operated, and throws a continuous stream. It is very effective
for watering shrubbery, gardens,
or lawns, and may be used in an
emergency as a fire extinguish-
er and prevent a conflagration.

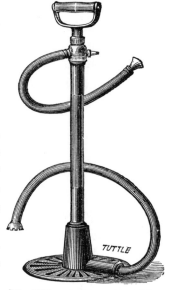

Fig. 125.—EXCELSIOR PUMP.

THE SIDNEY SEED-SOWER,
(Fig. 126).—This is a very useful implement, enabling

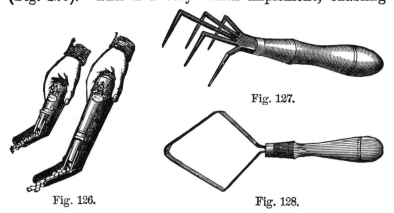

Fig. 127.

Fig. 126.   Fig. 128.

the operator to sow seeds with perfect regularity, especially in wet or windy weather. It will distribute large or

small seeds with equal regularity, either broadcast or in drills or pots.

THE EXCELSIOR WEEDING HOOK, (Fig. 127), is a very handy implement for removing weeds from among small and tender plants, and for stirring up the soil. It can be used between rows of seedlings, ornamental plants, or

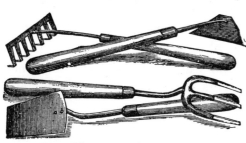

Fig. 129.—SMALL GARDEN SET.

wherever it is desirable to remove weeds, without injury to the plants or soiling the hands.

NOYES' HAND WEEDER, (Fig. 128), is a kind of miniature hand hoe, and is very convenient and useful for working between plants, dressing pots, and cleaning away weeds, where a large hoe could not be used to good advantage.

LADIES' AND CHILDRENS' GARDEN TOOLS, (Fig. 129).—In all flower gardens there is a great deal of hand-work to be done. This lot of small implements consisting of a spade, fork, rake, and hoe, will be found very useful in working on small flower borders.

Fig. 130.—STEP LADDER.

STEP LADDERS, (Fig. 130).—The step-ladder is always useful in a garden, especially during the fruiting season. It is made in different sizes, varying from three to ten

feet, and weighing from ten to thirty pounds ; it is made
with flat steps, so that a person may stand upon them
while working, and can be extended or contracted as required.   For use amongst large trees, in the orchard, a
much greater length of ladder is required, and there are
various forms of orchard ladders in use, but the step-
ladder is sufficient for all ordinary garden uses.

HAND-GLASSES.—The uses of these have been mentioned under cauliflowers, cucumber, etc.   Home-made

hand-glasses, being simply a
small frame covered with a pane
of glass, are very useful, but as
they exclude some light they
are not equal to those made with
glass all around.   Hand-glasses
with metal frames and glass
sides and top, are made of different sizes and styles, one of the

Fig. 131.—HAND GLASS.

more elaborate of which is shown in fig. 131.   Though
somewhat expensive, they will, if carefully used, last
many years.

Trellises, or supports for plants, are needed in the
flower and vegetable garden not only for climbers, but
for keeping plants which have weak
stems within proper bounds.   Trellises for pots may be purchased
ready-made, as may those for climb-
ing roses and such plants ; they are
usually made of rattan upon a frame
of light wooden stakes, and some
are made entirely of wire.   A person of a mechanical turn can
readily make all that will be need-

Fig. 132.

ed.   A few engravings are given here as suggestions.
Fig. 132 shows a useful support made with a barrel hoop
and staves ; the same plan may be carried out with two

or more hoops, and laths, if staves are too heavy. This will answer for tomatoes, raspberries, and various other plants. A more permanent tomato trellis is shown in fig. 133, in which slats are supported by Λ shaped uprights. If put together with screws, such a trellis may be carefully put away in the fall

Fig. 133.—TOMATO TRELLIS.

and made to last several years. A rustic trellis, like that in fig. 134, is often useful in the flower garden, or it may serve when covered with climbers to divide the flower from the vegetable garden. It is made of sticks of cedar or other durable wood, set as shown in the engraving, and tied where the bars cross one another with strong tarred twine. With these examples

Fig. 134.—RUSTIC TRELLIS.

as suggestions, one will find no difficulty in making more elaborate supports and with other materials.

MONTHLY CALENDAR OF OPERATIONS.

Although I have endeavored throughout the foregoing pages to be particular in stating the season or date at which each gardening operation should be done, still it may save time to the novice, and be otherwise of advantage, to briefly suggest what work should be done each month.

JANUARY.

GREENHOUSE AND FLOWER-GARDEN.—But little need now be done in either; in the greenhouse care must be exercised with the fires to protect against frost, as this is usually the coldest month of the year; it is also that in which there is the least sunshine. But little ventilating need be done, but when it does become necessary to do it, caution must be used; be careful to raise the ventilating sash only so high that the heated air from the greenhouse will be able to drive back the outer air to such an extent as not to chill the plants. For example, occasionally after a very cold night, where severe firing has been necessary to keep up the required temperature, say to 60°, it happens that the sun comes out bright during the following day, so that by noon or before, the temperature may be at 100° inside the greenhouse, though outside it may be nearly at zero; in such case the raising of the sashes an inch or two will rapidly lower the temperature of the greenhouse, so that an hour or so of such ventilating would be all that is required. If the greenhouse is heated by flue or even by hot water, examine nightly, that no combustible material is laid on the flue or thrown against the chimney of the boiler. As little fresh air can be given, insects are to be watched this month closely; by the use of fire heat a dry atmosphere will be created in which the *red spider* luxuriates; nothing answers so well for its destruction as copiously syringing the plants at night, and splashing the paths with water, as it cannot exist to an injurious extent in a moist atmosphere. The Aphis, or " green fly," must also be destroyed, or it will soon cause great injury to the plants. Tobacco in almost any form is death to it; it may be either used by burning the stems or dusted on as snuff, or syringed on in liquid form; for full directions see body of the work. Hyacinths and other bulbs that have been kept in cellar or other dark, cool place, may now be brought into the light of the greenhouse, provided they have filled the pots with roots, if not well rooted, leave them where they are until they are so, or select such of them as are best, and leave the others until ready.   In the outside flower-garden little can be done except that shrubs may be pruned, or new work, such as making walks or grading, if weather permits.

FRUIT-GARDEN.—Pruning, staking up, or mulching, can be done if the weather is such that the workman can stand out.   No plant is injured by being pruned in cold weather, though the pruner may be.

VEGETABLE GARDEN.—Nothing can be done this month in the northern states except to prepare manure, and get sashes, tools, etc., in working order, but in sections of the country where there is but little or no frost, the hardier kinds of seeds and plants may be sown and planted, such as asparagus, cabbage, cauliflower, carrot, leek, lettuce, onion, parsnip, peas, spinach, turnip, etc., etc. In any section where these seeds can be sown in the open ground, it is an indication that hot-beds may be begun for the sowing of such tender vegetables as tomatoes, egg and pepper plants, etc., though unless in the extreme southern states, hot-beds had better not be started before the first of February.

FEBRUARY.

GREENHOUSE AND FLOWER-GARDEN.—The directions for January will in the main apply to this month, except that now some of the hardier annuals may be sown, and also the propagation of plants by cuttings may be done rather better now than in January, for instructions in such matters, see chapter on Propagation.

FRUIT-GARDEN.—But little can be done in most of the northern states as yet, and in sections where there is no frost in the ground, it is likely to be too wet to work, but in many southern states this will be the best month for planting fruit-trees and plants of all kinds, particularly strawberries, raspberries, blackberries, pear and apple, while grape-vines will do quite a month later.   One of the greatest wants in many parts of the south is reliable nurseries, where such things can be procured, and as all such plants are at this season frozen solid in nurseries at the north, orders for such things cannot usually be shipped before April; still though something may be lost by this circumstance, if proper attention is given to planting, watering, and shading, (when practicable), good results may be obtained, as it is always better to take plants of any kind from a cold climate to a hot one, than from a hot to a cold.

VEGETABLE GARDEN.—Horse manure, leaves from the woods, or refuse hops from the breweries, when they can be obtained, may be got together towards the latter part of the month and mixed and turned to get " sweetened" preparatory to forming hot-beds; for detailed instructions see article on hot-beds. Manure that is to be used for the crops should be turned and broken up as fine as possible, for it should be known that the more completely manure of any kind can be mixed with the soil, the better will be the crop, and of course if it is dug or plowed-in in large unbroken lumps, it cannot be properly commingled.

MARCH.

GREENHOUSE AND FLOWER-GARDEN.—Brighter sunshine and longer days will now begin to show their effects by a rapid growth of plants in the greenhouse, and also in those of the parlor or window garden ; examine all plants that are growing vigorously and are healthy, and if the roots have struck to the sides of the pot and matted the " ball " of earth, then they must be shifted into larger sized pots; if this is long neglected the plants are certain to suffer in consequence; for details of operations see chapter on Potting. The plants propagated last month may now need shifting also, and propagation should continue of all plants that are likely to be wanted. If propagation is put off later, most plants would not be large enough if needed for bedding purposes in the flower-garden in summer. The hardier kinds of annuals may now be sown ; it is best done in boxes, as recommended elsewhere. Lawns may now be raked off and top-dressed with short manure or rich garden earth where manure is not obtainable, and on light soils flower-beds may be dug up so as to forward the work preparatory to the coming of the busy season.

FRUIT-GARDEN.—In light, dry soils planting may be safely done in many sections, but we again caution the inexperienced not to get impatient and begin to plant before the ground is dry ; it is bad to do so even in light sandy soils, but in stiff and clayey ones it will be utter destruction. Again at this season, although a tree or plant will receive no injury *when its roots are in the soil*, should a frost come after planting, yet that same amount of freezing would greatly injure the plant if the roots were uncovered and exposed. Thousands of trees and plants fail every year from this cause; they are exposed for sale in our markets with no protection to the roots, and even the experienced purchaser rarely has sufficient knowledge to be certain whether the roots of a tree have been injured by being frozen or dried up by the cold winds of March. It is always best when it can be done, to purchase direct from the nearest reliable nurserymen; they well know the importance of having the roots properly protected, while in two cases out of three the market huckster neither knows nor cares.

VEGETABLE GARDEN.—This is a busy month. Hot-beds must now be all started, and all the seeds of the hardier vegetables may be sown in locations where the frost is out and the ground dry, the list given for southern states in January may now be used at the north, while for most of the southern states the tender kinds of vegetables may now be sown and planted, such as egg-plant, okra, melon, sweet potatoes, squash, tomatoes, potatoes, etc.

APRIL.

GREENHOUSE AND FLOWER-GARDEN.—Plants whether grown in greenhouse or in windows, will require increased ventilation and water this month, and as they will now be growing rapidly, due attention must be paid to shifting into larger pots when necessary, and also increase the space if possible by putting the hardier sorts out in frames. If plants are crowded at this season in the greenhouse, they will grow spindling and weak. It is better to throw away the common or coarser plants if there is not room for the finer sorts to develop properly. Towards the end of the month it may be necessary to partially shade the glass of the greenhouse; this may be either done by sheeting hung on rollers from the top, or more simply and cheaply by making a very thin whitewash of lime; this may be spattered over the glass very lightly at first, just to mark the glass with white spots as thick as if a slight shower should leave the marks of its drops. The wash is to be spattered on thicker every week or two, as the season advances. The planting of all kinds of hardy herbaceous plants and shrubs may now be done in the flower-garden. Bulbs and all tender plants that have been covered for protection in winter may now be stripped, and the beds slightly forked and raked. Sow tender annual flower seeds in boxes.

FRUIT-GARDEN.—Strawberries that have been covered up by straw or leaves, should now be relieved around the plant, only leaving the covering between the plants; see chapter on Strawberries. Raspberries, grape-vines, etc., that have been laid down may now be uncovered and tied up to stakes or trellises, and all new plantations of these and other fruits should now be made.

VEGETABLE GARDEN.—The covering of asparagus, rhubarb, spinach, etc., should now be removed, and the beds hoed or dug lightly. The hardier sorts of vegetable seeds and plants, such as beets, cabbage, cauliflower, celery, lettuce, onions, parsley, parsnip, peas, potatoes, radishes, spinach, turnip, etc., should all be sown or planted by the middle of the month, if the soil is dry and warm, and in all cases where practicable before the end of the month, for if these varieties of vegetables are delayed until the hot weather in May, they will not be so early, and in most cases will not produce so fine a crop. It is quite a common practice with many amateurs to delay garden operations of all kinds until May, but all the hardier sorts of vegetables are likely to be later and inferior in consequence. Any one expecting to get early cabbage, lettuce, or radishes, if planting or sowing is delayed until the time of planting tomato and egg plants in May, is certain to be disappointed.

MAY.

GREENHOUSE AND FLOWER-GARDEN.—The majority of plants in the greenhouse or window garden should now be in their finest bloom. Firing may now be entirely dispensed with in the greenhouse, though care must yet be exercised in ventilating in the first part of the month, as we still have cold winds in this section. By the end of the month all of the plants that are wanted for the summer decoration of the flower borders may be planted out. In doing so, when the ball of earth has been completely matted with roots, it will be better to bruise it slightly between the hands, so that the water will pass freely through the " ball," as it often happens that it is so hard and dry as to prevent the water from penetrating it, and the growth is impeded in consequence. Water copiously after planting if the weather is dry. When the greenhouse is not to be used during the summer months, camellias, azaleas, and plants of that character should be set out-doors under partial shade, but most of the other plants usually kept in the greenhouse or window garden in winter, may be set in the open border, where the pots should be plunged to the rim in ashes or sand, keeping them slightly apart from each other, to prevent crowding. Where there are indications that the pot has become filled with roots, the plant should be shifted into a size larger just as it is done inside

the greenhouse ; as the plants make growth, they with few exceptions should be pinched back to cause a stout and branching
form.   Lawns should now be mown and edgings trimmed
nicely, and all flower-beds hoed and raked, for if weeds are not
kept down as they first appear, treble the labor will be required to
eradicate them next month.   Annuals that have been sown in the
greenhouse or hot-bed may now be planted out, and seeds of such
sorts as Mignonette, Sweet Alyssum, Phlox Drummondii, Portulaca, etc., etc., may be sown in the borders.

FRUIT-GARDEN.—Where it has not been convenient before, most
of the smaller fruits may yet be planted the first part of the month.
Ply the hoe vigorously to keep down weeds.   If any of the numerous varieties of caterpillars, slugs, or worms make their appearance on the young shoots of vines or trees, a free application of
tobacco dust will dislodge most of them.   It is best to use it as a
preventive, for if they once get a foothold, the crop may be ruined.

VEGETABLE GARDEN.—Thin out all crops sown last month,
that are now large enough, and hoe deeply all planted crops, such
as cabbage, cauliflower, lettuce, etc.   Plant out all tender vegetables, viz: tomatoes, egg and pepper plants, sweet potatoes, etc.
Plant seeds of lima beans, corn, melons, okra, cucumbers, etc., and
succession crops of peas, spinach, lettuce, beans, etc.

JUNE.

GREEEHOUSE AND FLOWER-GARDEN.—The greenhouse may
now be used for hot-house or tropical plants, if such are desired during the summer months.   It should now be well shaded
and fine specimens of fancy caladiums, dracænas, palms, ferns,
and such plants as are grown for their beauty of foliage will make
it very attractive.   Hyacinths, Tulips, and other spring bulbs may
now be dug up, dried, and placed away for next fall's planting,
and their places filled with such plants as Coleus, Achyranthes,
and the various " white-leaved plants " that are suited for late bedding.   Lawns will now require to be mowed weekly in all well-
kept places.   It is as much an indication of slovenliness to see a
door-yard that has any pretensions to be called a lawn, with the
grass uncut, as it would be to see a dust begrimed carpet in the
parlor.

FRUIT-GARDEN.—If strawberries have not been mulched with
hay or straw in winter, the cut grass from the lawn is a convenient
thing to place between the rows to keep the fruit from getting

sanded by dashing rains. Nearly all the small fruits, such as gooseberries, raspberries, etc., etc., are much improved by having a mulching of some sort placed around the roots, which should be done this month.

VEGETABLE GARDEN.—This is usually the busiest month in the garden, crops mature and have to be gathered, and while doing so, weeds are apt to steal a march on you, and may destroy entirely some of your hard work of former months, unless you attack them in their embryo stage, that is just when breaking through the soil. A man will hoe and rake over six times the surface of soil when the weeds are in this stage that he would if weeds were six inches high, and in this matter more than anything else I know of in gardening, does a "stitch in time save nine." Beans, peas, beets, corn, cucumbers, lettuce, etc., may yet be sown for succession crops, and late plantings of Irish potatoes and sweet potatoes will yet do well on suitable soils. Tomatoes should be tied up to trellises or stakes, if fine flavored and handsome fruit is desired.

JULY.

GREENHOUSE AND FLOWER-GARDEN.—But little may be said of the greenhouse this month. Watering, ventilating, and fumigating, (or the use of tobacco in other forms for destruction of aphis), must be attended to. Keep the atmosphere of the greenhouse moist. The plants from the greenhouse that may have been plunged out-doors, must be watched when they require repotting, and where the roots have run through the pots, they should also be occasionally turned round, to break them off, for if this is not done now, it would seriously injure the plant in fall when the roots have run through the pot and deep into the soil, as they often do. Plants such as dahlias, roses, gladioluses, as well as many herbaceous perennial and annual plants, will now require staking; be careful to proportion the size of the stake to that of the plant, and do not tie it too tightly. Stakes painted green look best, and the square are nearly as good as the round ones, and much cheaper. Carnations and other plants that are throwing up flower-stems, if wanted to flower in winter, should be cut back.

FRUIT-GARDEN.—If there are any signs of mildew on the grape-vine leaves, dust them over with dry sulphur, choosing a still, warm day. The fruit will now be gathered from the strawberry vines, and if new beds are to be formed, the system recommended of layering the plants in small pots is the best; see Strawberries.

Where apples, pears, peaches, etc., have set fruit thickly, thin out one-half or two-thirds of the young fruit, as by doing so you will get at least an equal weight and much finer fruit. The same is true of grape-vines and all other fruits that have set thickly; where thinning out is practicable, it will always be beneficial to practice it.

VEGETABLE GARDEN.—Plants of cabbages, cauliflowers, celery, and all similar varieties of vegetables wanted for fall or winter use are best planted this month, though in some sections they will do if left until next. See directions given under these separate heads. Sweet corn, beans, cucumbers and lettuce may yet be planted for late crops, and in some sections ruta-baga turnips for the main winter crop. Tomatoes should be kept tied up to stakes or trellises, and sweet potatoes must be hoed so as to prevent the vines rooting at the joints.

AUGUST.

GREENHOUSE AND FLOWER-GARDEN.—The instructions for July apply with but little variation in these departments this month.

FRUIT-GARDEN.—Strawberries that were planted in spring, and also those that have fruited will now be making "runners" or young plants freely. All runners should be kept cut off close to the old plant, so that the full force of the root is expended in maturing the "crowns" or fruit buds of the next season's crop. If plants are wanted for fresh plantations, about the required number can be allowed to run, but should be layered in pots, as recommended under Strawberries. Cut away the old stems of raspberries and blackberries that have borne their fruit, and thin out the young shoots to three or four canes to each hill or plant, if tied to stakes and topped when 4 or 5 feet high, they will make stronger canes for fruiting next year.

VEGETABLE GARDEN.—Planted crops, such as cabbage, cauliflower, and celery, should be hoed deeply. We do not recommend the earthing up of celery this month. Onions will in many sections now be ready for harvesting; this condition will be known by the tops becoming yellow and falling down; they are best dried by placing them in some dry shed in thin layers. For sweet potatoes, see directions of last month. Spinach may be sown for early fall use, but it is yet too early to sow for the winter crop. Red-top, White Globe, and Yellow Aberdeen turnips should

11

now be sown. Ruta-baga turnips sown last month will need thinning.

SEPTEMBER.

GREENHOUSE AND FLOWER-GARDEN.—Towards the end of the month in many sections, the more tender plants will require to be put in the greenhouse, or housed in some way, but be careful to keep them as cool as possible during the day; they would be better outside yet if it was safe to risk them. Cuttings of all bedding plants may now be made freely, if wanted for next season, as the young cuttings rooted in fall make better plants for next spring's use than the old plants. This is true of what is known as bedding plants, such as geraniums, fuchsias, verbenas, heliotropes, etc., etc. But with roses and other plants of a woody nature, the old plants are usually the best. Holland bulbs, such as hyacinths, tulips, etc., etc., and most of the varieties of lilies may be planted this month; see detailed instructions under Holland Bulbs. Violets that are wanted for winter will now be growing freely, and the runners should be trimmed off as recommended for strawberries last month. Seeds of pansies, daisies, mignonette, sweet alyssum, candytuft, etc., should now be sown in the early part of the month.

FRUIT-GARDEN.—New plantations of strawberry plants may now be made from the runners that have been layered in pots; the sooner in the month they are planted, the stronger they will be for next season; these plants will soon make runners that must be trimmed off to throw the strength into the crowns for next season's fruiting. Attend to raspberries and blackberries as advised last month, if not then done.

VEGETABLE GARDEN.—Seeds of cabbage, cauliflower, and lettuce to raise plants to be placed in cold frames, should be sown in this latitude from the 10th to the 20th of this month; the main crop of spinach or sprouts that is wanted for winter or spring use, should be sown about same dates. Celery may now have the earth drawn to it with the hoe preparatory to earthing-up by the spade. Onions that were not dried and harvested last month, must be done this, or it will be too late. The early or flat sorts of turnips may yet be sown the first week of this month.

OCTOBER.

GREENHOUSE AND FLOWER-GARDEN.—In almost all northern localities, all tender plants yet outside should be got under cover the early part of this month. Avoid the use of fire heat as long as possible; unless the nights become cold enough to chill the plants inside of the house, they are better without fire heat. When there is indication that the night is likely to be cold, let down the sashes that have been raised for ventilation, early in the afternoon, and thus shut up the heated air until next day. If there is a cold frame or pit at hand, the hardier sorts of plants, such as roses, carnations, camellias, azaleas, etc., will do better if placed there until middle of November, than in the ordinary greenhouse. Treated in this manner they make strong, healthy roots, that enable them to withstand the forcing process better when placed in the greenhouse. Look out for and destroy insects; see methods already given. The planting of fall bulbs of all kinds may continue during this month. Dahlias, tuberoses, gladiolus, cannas, caladiums, tigridias, and all tender bulbs or tubers that are planted in spring, should be taken up before the end of the month, dried and stowed away in some place free from frost during winter.

FRUIT-GARDEN.—Strawberries that have been layered in pots may yet be planted this month; great care should be taken to trim off runners from early plantings. All kinds of fruit-trees and shrubs may be set out; if planting is deferred to the last of the month, the ground around the roots should be mulched to the thickness of three or four inches, with leaves, straw, or rough manure, as a protection to the roots against the frost.

VEGETABLE GARDEN.—This is one of the busiest fall months in the kitchen garden, celery will now be in full growth, and will require close attention to earthing-up, and during the last part of the month, the first lot may be stored away in trenches for winter; see Celery; beets, carrots, parsnips, squash, sweet potatoes, and all other roots not designed to be left in the ground during winter, should be dug by the end of the month. The cabbage, cauliflower, and lettuce plants from the seed sown about the middle of last month, should now be pricked out in cold frames. If lettuce is wanted for winter use, it may be now planted in the greenhouse, and will be ready for use by Christmas. Rhubarb and asparagus, if wanted for use in winter, should be taken up in large clumps and stowed away in pit, frame, shed, or cellar for a month or two, when it may be taken into the greenhouse and packed closely together under the stage, and will be fit for use from **January to March**, according to the temperature of the house.

NOVEMBER.

GREENHOUSE AND FLOWER-GARDEN.—All plants should now be in-doors; a sharp look-out must be kept for cold snaps. These often come very unexpectedly in November, and as many plants are injured by frost in this as there are in the colder months, when the enemy is more closely watched for. When fire heat is freely used, be careful to keep up the proper supply of moisture by syringing, sprinkling the paths, etc. In the flower-garden nothing is now to be done except to clean off dead stalks and straw up tender roses, vines, etc., and wherever there is time, to dig up and rake the borders, as it will greatly facilitate spring work. All beds where hyacinths or other fall bulbs have been planted, had better be covered with rough litter or leaves to the depth of two or three inches. If short, thoroughly decayed manure can be spared, a good sprinkling spread over the lawn will help it to a finer growth in spring.

FRUIT-GARDEN.—In cold sections the hay or straw mulching recommended in the chapter on the Strawberry may be put on during the last of this month. Grape-vines and fruit-trees generally should be pruned, and if wood of the vine is wanted for cuttings, or cions of fruit-trees for grafts, they should be tied in small neat bunches and buried in the ground until spring.

VEGETABLE GARDEN.—All celery that is to be stored for winter use, should be put away before the end of the month in all places north of Richmond, Va.; south of that it may be left in most places in the rows where grown if covered up. Directions for storing celery for winter are given under Celery. The stalks of asparagus beds should be cut over, and as asparagus sometimes becomes a weed, it is better to burn the stems if there are berries on them. Spread a heavy dressing of rough manure three or four inches thick on the beds. All roots that are yet in the ground and not designed to be left there all winter, must be dug up in this latitude before the middle of the month, or they may be frozen in until spring; onions, spinach, sprouts, cabbage, or lettuce plants that are outside should be covered with two or three inches of leaves, salt hay, or straw, to protect during winter. Cabbages that have headed may be usually preserved against injury by frost until the middle of next month, by simply pulling them up and packing them close together in a dry spot in the open field with the *heads down*, and roots up; on the approach of cold weather in December, they should be covered up with leaves as high as the tops of the roots, or if the soil is light, it may be thrown over them if leaves are not convenient; cabbages so packed will keep until March, if the covering has not been put on too early. Whenever it is practicable, all empty ground should be dug or plowed this month, trenching or subsoiling whenever time will permit. All such operations when performed in the fall, not only benefit the soil, but greatly facilitate work at the hurried season in the spring. The cold frames where cabbage, lettuce, or cauliflower plants have been planted will now require regular ventilation by lifting up the sashes in warm days, and on the approach of very cold weather, straw mats or shutters would be a great protection to the plants; for the cauliflower this protection is absolutely necessary here.

DECEMBER.

GREENHOUSE AND FLOWER-GARDEN.—We are now fairly into winter, and close attention must be given to protecting all tender plants. It is one of the commonest complaints, especially from ladies, that their plants " looked so nice until one cold night in December " defeated the whole care of the year by killing or wounding hundreds of the cherished favorites of the greenhouse or window garden. There is no rule but vigilance, and as extra strong fires will be kept up, look out again nightly for all combustible matter near the flue or chimney. If you find the thermometer in the greenhouse or parlor where your plants are kept, falling down to 34 or 35 degrees, the chances are that there will be frost in the house; the best protection in such cases is either to set the plants under the benches or on the walk if in the greenhouse, or move them from the cold point if in the parlor; if the plants are low and uniform in hight, covering them with paper or sheeting will usually save them from injury even if the thermometer falls to 26 or 28 degrees. Another plan is to dash water on the pipes or flue in the greenhouse on cold nights, the steam arises to the glass, freezes there, and stops up all crevices. All mulching, strawing up, or other modes of protecting against frost in use in the flower-garden, must be finished this month.

FRUIT-GARDEN.—Grape-vines, raspberries, etc., in sections where protection from severe frost is of advantage, should be attended to this month, by laying them down as near the ground as possible, and covering them with rough litter or leaves, or with a few inches of soil.

VEGETABLE GARDEN.—The final covering of celery in trenches,

or roots in pits; the spinach crop in ground, or any other article in need of protection, must have it done before the end of this month.   Manure and compost heaps should now be forwarded as rapidly as possible, and turned and mixed so as to be in proper condition for spring.   Snow that accumulates on cold frames or other glass structures, should be removed, particularly if the soil that the glass covers was not frozen before the snow fell; if frozen, it may remain on the sashes longer, for the plants if frozen are, of course dormant, and would not be injured by being deprived of light for eight or ten days.

INDEX.

PRACTICAL FLORICULTURE;

A Guide to the Successful Propagation and Cultivation

OF

FLORISTS' PLANTS.

BY PETER HENDERSON, BERGEN CITY, N. J.,

AUTHOR OF "GARDENING FOR PROFIT."

———•◦•———

MR. HENDERSON is known as the largest Commercial Florist in the country. In the present work he gives a full account of his modes of propagation and cultivation. It is adapted to the wants of the amateur, as well as the professional grower.

The scope of the work may be judged from the following

TABLE OF CONTENTS.

Beautifully Illustrated. Sent post-paid. Price, $1.50.

ORANGE JUDD COMPANY,

751 Broadway, New-York.